changing rooms

handy andy's weekend workbook

changing rooms

handy andy's weekend workbook

Andy Kane and Chris Short

BBC

contents

tools, rules and timber

bedrooms

reception rooms

kitchens and bathrooms

welcome

Okay, let me guess. You're either reading this book because you really want to tackle some DIY projects and just need a bit of motivation, or you're reading this book because everyone else wants you to tackle some DIY projects and you just need a bit of peace and quiet. Either way, you're in safe hands. For the cool tool enthusiast there's a load of great projects to get started on straightaway, but for those of you who need a bit more time 'building up to speed' there's a good few pages of dead simple and dead useful information to browse through first.

I've taken all the projects in this book from the *Changing Rooms* TV series. That's the one where two designers with a very limited budget spend two days helping two couples redecorate each others' rooms while they're out. Sounds strange? Too right. And it may seem stranger still that I'm now suggesting you spend your weekends copying DIY projects that have been devised to work for very little money and in very little time, but that is exactly the beauty of this whole book. The point is that whatever ridiculous idea they rope me into while we're filming, you can bet that the only way it gets done in time is for me to come up with a construction plan that is simple, quick and foolproof. And if I've learnt one thing in my time as a self-employed carpenter, it's how to get a decent job done quickly and easily. So that's what you've got here – a book full of the best ideas for the best projects, made the best way, and all of them tested in someone else's house first. Magic!

Now if you're a confirmed DIYphobic, you probably think this 'homebuilt' nonsense is all far more trouble than it's worth (you'd rather just call a spade a spade, a screwdriver a cocktail drink and let that be an end to it). Well, you'd be wrong to do that and I hope this book might actually prove to be the beginning of that realization. Not only is a spot of DIY far easier and far more fun than you'd imagine, it's also the only affordable way you can actually end up with exactly what you want, as opposed to the nearest equivalent from the local superstore. Best of all, there's no substitute for that great feeling you get when you stand back to admire a finished piece of work and say, 'Yeah, I did that.' At the end of the day, all DIY building projects can be divided into three basic stages, which I call the three 'Fs'. The first is 'Fabricating', when you've got to make the bits; the second is 'Fixing', when you stick them together; and the final one is 'Finishing', when you make the whole thing look decent. That's it. Trust me, I'm a carpenter.

If you've got the time now, have a flick through the rest of this book and get a feel for the kind of projects that are in it. They're all arranged in three sections – bedrooms, reception rooms and kitchens/bathrooms – so you can quickly see how they might feature in your own place. All of them will work a treat and none of them will use more than a few hours of your time and some fairly basic tools and materials. If you're still unsure whether all this is for you, just try out a couple of the simpler projects first and get the feel of working with wood. It's truly amazing stuff and not just for making books!

how to use this book

This book has 38 brilliant projects in it, all of them proven to work and pretty easy to make. Ironically, not a single one of them may be right for you, but don't panic – it's meant to be like that.

These projects were all created as genuine solutions to genuine problems, but as they were designed to fit someone else's home, there's no guarantee that all the dimensions will be right for your place. Chances are, though, that most of the projects in the book can be copied screw for screw and when you've finished you'll end up with something you're absolutely delighted with.

But that's just the beginning of the story. It starts with you getting to grips with some of the most popular DIY tools and techniques and develops to the point where you consult this book more for inspiration than instruction. Each turn of the page will set you off on a train of thought geared around your specific needs. What I'm saying is give the book some time and enthusiasm and it will inspire you to come up with projects for yourself. Ultimately it will enable you to create pretty much whatever you want.

Now before you dive into the projects themselves, there are a few things you should read first. Most important is the section on safety (pages 154–5). This will help you to use all the tools, timber and techniques described on pages 12–32 (more essential reading) with well-placed confidence. In Tools, Rules and Timber there are some universal construction techniques which will crop up again and again in projects throughout this book (for example, using a plugged screw to fix your project to a wall, pages 28–29) so take some time to read them here first. Once you've read this section and everything seems fairly obvious, you're ready to tackle anything in this book. And if you have any trouble with imperial or metric measurements while you are working on a project, you'll find a handy conversion chart on page 157.

Always remember – the more familiar you are with the rules, the easier it is to bend them to your advantage. If you eventually master every-thing I tell you, I guarantee that there won't be a single project in this book that you can't adapt exactly to your needs.

TOOLS, RULES & TIMBER

This book is for people who dabble in DIY as a pleasure, not as a penance, so I'm not going to waste your time with a lot of tedious facts and figures that you'll probably never need to know. Over the next few pages is some pretty straightforward information about the basic kit you'll need to tackle the projects that follow, and some tips and techniques on how to make sure they turn out just the way you want. If you're already 'DIY literate', get stuck into the rest of the book right now – you can always come back to this section if you hit a problem, or while you're waiting for the glue to dry...

tooling up

It's quite easy to go out and spend a small fortune on DIY tools and still end up with the wrong screwdriver when you next need to change a plug. You don't need a vanload of hardware just to put up a shelf, but you do need to spend some time making sure that you build up your tool kit so that it will meet your immediate needs and also grow with your future ambitions. The most common accidents in DIY are caused by someone trying to 'make do' with the wrong tool, so know what your kit is capable of and don't go beyond those limits. Use the right tool, as advised for each project, and read the safety information on pages 154–5 before you start.

THE BASIC KIT

Even if the nearest thing you have to a DIY tool kit is the contents of your cutlery drawer, don't despair. For the price of a meal out you can equip yourself with a perfectly decent set-up that will enable you to tackle most of the projects in this book safely and success-fully. In my experience, when you are buying tools it's always better to go for the quality brands that will last, rather than buying a lot of cheaper stuff all in one go.

BEVEL-EDGED CHISELS – You'll need a couple of sizes and you'll need to keep them clean and sharp. Chisels are shaped (bevelled) at the point for a reason: flat side down they'll dig deeper and deeper into the wood as you go, the other way up they won't. Let them go blunt and they'll be useless either way.

BRADAWL – A what? This little spike is dead useful. Not only can you use it to mark holes for drilling, you can also use it to push pilot holes into soft wood for screws. And if you happen to lose your pencil, it also makes great scratches for cutting along.

CRAFT KNIFE – Get a knife with interchangeable or disposable blades so that it's sharp when you need it, and ideally one with a retracting system to keep blades safely out of the way when you've finished.

EXPANDING RULE – An absolute essential for accurately measuring all manner of materials. It doesn't need to be that long – a 2.4m (8ft) sheet of MDF (see page 18) is usually the biggest thing you'll have to cope with – but it does need to be easy to spot, as it will be the first thing you lose when the dust starts to fly.

HAMMER – Claw hammers look like fun, but you'll get far more use out of a smaller pin hammer to begin with. This is for knocking in panel pins to hold joints together while the glue dries. Get one with a flattened end so that you can work with all sizes of nails.

HANDSAW – Buy a decent one and look after it. Keep the teeth clean and dry when you're not using it, and use either saw-setting pliers or ask the guys at the hardware shop to sharpen it when sawing seems to be all sweat and no progress.

Below: A basic tool kit contains less than a dozen items, but buy good-quality ones and they'll last you forever. Clockwise from top centre: sandpaper, craft knife, expanding rule, elecric drill, screwdrivers, bradawl, pin hammer, chisels, handsaw, spirit level, set square.

POWER DRILL/DRIVER – The most expensive bit of the whole kit I'm afraid, but as useful as all the others put together. A high specification drill/driver (ideally with hammer action for boring into stubborn masonry) and a good selection of bits and heads will act as both drill and screwdriver and rarely leave your hand. Get the best one you can and prepare for a long-term relationship.

SANDPAPER – This comes in various grades but it's essentially like a hangover – the rough ones do the most damage. If you're not using it on a power sander, you'll need a little block of wood to wrap it around for maximum comfort and effect.

SCREWDRIVERS – Unfortunately, there seems to be a conspiracy among the screw manufac-

turers of this world that makes it impossible to have one screwdriver to fit everything! However, you can now get hold of screwdriver sets where a number of different heads clip into the same handle. This reduces the frustration considerably.

SPIRIT LEVEL – Get a decent one so that you know it's absolutely accurate and then use it at every possible opportunity. You don't need a particularly big one as you can always rest it on a straight piece of timber to span long gaps. However, just make sure the piece of timber is indeed straight, or be prepared for the consequences.

TRY SQUARE OR SET SQUARE – Great for marking straight cuts across planks and essential for keeping 90° cuts and corners square.

ADVANCED KIT

So now you've got the bug, what are you going to buy next? Step right this way... Here are a few trinkets which won't just open up new doors, they'll actually help you build them. You certainly don't need all these in one go, but each tool you buy will allow you to tackle an ever increasing range of homebuilt projects. Once again, take your time to invest, and buy something that's going to cope with whatever tasks you may ask of it in the future.

CRAMPS – Or clamps, depending on where you're from. A few of these will save hours of fiddling about trying to hold materials together while you work. It's like having an extra pair of hands without having to explain what you want them to do all the time. Sash cramps have an enormous reach and are invaluable for holding several planks of wood together while they glue to form something like a new tabletop or kitchen worksurface (see scrap timber worksurface, page 146).

JIGSAW – It's not in the basic kit, but this would be the first thing I'd buy beyond it. Probably too brutal for the more delicate cuts, but I'd hate to be faced with a huge sheet of uncut MDF without one. There are different blades for cutting different materials,

THERE'S A PLACE FOR EVERYTHING

There are two very good reasons for storing your tools in a clean and organized environment. First, you know that whenever you reach out for something it's going to work properly. Tools are precision instruments, even if you are not. Keep them in good nick and they'll serve you well for years. Second, you know that whenever you reach out for something it's actually going to be there. There is nothing more frustrating than having to stop in the middle of a job to go and look for the right tool. That's when you get tempted to 'make do' and that's when the problems start.

Left: An advanced tool kit. Clockwise from top left: plane, router, power drill, sliding bevel, mole grips, power sander, cramps, mitre block, jigsaw.

so don't just dump the first pack you see into the trolley. If you intend to be cutting long straight runs of timber or board far more than curves or short sections, then you might be better buying a powered circular saw rather than a jigsaw.

MITRE BLOCK – This very simple tool is decep-tively useful. A mitre is simply a way of join-ing two bits of timber where they meet at a corner. The two ends are cut at 45° and then secured to form a 90° angle. Take a look at the corners of your nearest picture frame to see what I mean. A mitre block is simply a tool for working up the angles without resorting to a ruler, a protractor and a degree in engineering. All you need do for an accurate join is sit your timber into the mitre block and then saw it using the 45° slots in the block as a guide. They're not expensive to buy, but making one of your own could be your very first project!

MOLE GRIPS – Not a wrestling hold, but a sur-prisingly useful little gadget. These things are

like the love child from a pair of pliers and a clamp. The adjustable jaws can be set to different widths and then locked into position: great for holding bits of timber together while you fix them with glue or screws.

PLANE – Planes are used to cut away wood and leave a lovely smooth finish where there is just too much work for a sander to cope with. You can get hand-powered ones if you want that traditional feel of craftsmanship, or electric ones if you want to be finished by nightfall. Either way, there is nothing like the touch of smooth planed timber.

POWER SANDER – Not essential, but certainly worth while if you're planning on smoothing down some large areas, such as a door or a tabletop. They make big square ones for big square surfaces and little pointy ones for tricky corners, so work out where it's going to get most use before you buy one. A floor sander is essential for preparing your floor-boards before painting (see colour-washed floorboards, page 74).

ROUTER– With a selection of various shaped bits and some basic techniques, this brilliant 'toy' will let you do all the little grooves and ornate edges in timber and boards that suddenly make your homebuilt projects look very professional indeed. If you want to turn the front of all your shelves into fancy-looking decorative mouldings, this is the baby to do it with. The router also comes into its own when making slots for projects like the magic shelves on page 66.

SLIDING BEVEL – This unusual instrument of torture is actually designed so that you can measure odd angles and then transfer those dimensions to the wood for cutting. Invaluable when you're working away from the comfort of 90° and 45° angles.

planks and boards

Whole trees are tricky to get into the car, so I advise you to buy your timber cut to size. Planks are the most usual way of buying plain and simple timber, but there is now a whole range of artificially constructed wood fibre boards on the market. For my money, these just keep getting better in terms of cost and practicality. Follow the golden rule and use planks where you're going to see the wood grain as part of the finished project, and manmade board where you're not.

WOOD GLORIOUS WOOD

There is no doubt about it, timber is gorgeous stuff – great to work with and great to look at; indeed, you would be hard pressed to find anything that is more attractive and adaptable. Add to this the fact that you can mould it into the most intricate shapes with the simplest of tools, and then sit back and enjoy the results of your labour for years and years, and you have what must be nigh on the perfect material. Best of all, it really does grow on trees...

There are endless varieties of timber to choose from, but basically they all fall into two categories – hardwood and softwood. Hardwood takes forever to grow and gives you the most wonderful fine-grained patterns as a result. It's normally used for projects where the natural timber is going to be on show for ever, and the quality of the work is directly dependent on the quality of the raw material itself. With a few minor exceptions, all hardwood comes from deciduous trees, which lose their leaves in winter (elm, oak, beech, etc.), while softwood comes from the classic coniferous trees which stay green all year round (pine, fir, spruce, etc.). Hardwood also takes for ever to replace, so unless you can be absolutely sure your wood is coming from a 'renewable source', don't come running to me when your grand-children ask you where all the deciduous trees have gone... Softwood is not only far easier to work with, it's also far quicker to

grow and, as a result, far cheaper to buy. There is nothing in this book that cannot be constructed in softwood, and that's no bad thing.

Timber comes in all sorts of shapes and sizes, but many suppliers will now cut it down to roughly the measurements you require before you leave the shop. Better still, get to know all the regular sizes that are available 'off the shelf' and then, where possible, plan the dimensions of your projects with those in mind. You can get softwood timber from all the big DIY super-stores now, but you might have to search out a local timber merchant if you are determined to get some hardwood planks. Because timber is full of moisture when it's alive, it takes some time to dry out once it's been cut. While it dries, it can twist or warp, so make sure the straight, flat planks you select from the timber merchant or DIY shed are truly straight and flat before you pay for them. When sorting through softwood, go for the timber that has the tightest growth rings. This means it's from the middle of the trunk and that's where trees hide their best wood. Also, try to avoid anything with a lot of knot holes in it – they're a real pain to cut or drill. The timber you buy will usually be one of two types of finish, sawn or planed. Sawn timber has a rough surface but comes out at the exact size quoted on the label. Planed timber is a little more expensive than sawn but doesn't have to be sanded down before you paint or oil it. However, be warned: your planed timber may be a little bit smaller than the dimensions advertised, which may still refer to its sawn size.

From bottom left to top right: planed timber, sawn timber and hardwood.

BOARD STIFF

More and more popular and widely available in all the DIY sheds and timber merchants, manufactured boards come in a huge variety and can be used in many homebuilt projects. These sheets of material are often fabricated from the pulped timber that would once have been thrown away as waste, making them both brown and green simultaneously: very PC. The boards come in sizes anything up to 2.4x1.2m (8x4ft), but as a rule they are not great on tensile strength. In other words, long bits without any support in the middle will bend and snap once you put any significant weight on them, so make sure you use the right material for the job. The main types you are likely to come into contact with are MDF, hardboard, chipboard and plywood. These, and other varieties of fibreboard, are described below, of these MDF definitely gets my nomination for most useful material award.

CHIPBOARD – Although basically a sheet of old wood chips glued together and pressed flat, this board is far stronger than it sounds. You will often find it as shelves, or lurking under the colourful veneers of your kitchen worktops. Chipboard has very good tensile strength for unsupported load-bearing, but it eats normal saw bits for breakfast, so you'll need a tungsten carbide-tipped blade to get through it.

HARDBOARD – This is the thin brown stuff you usually find under your carpets and lino. It's very poor for load-bearing duties, but it is very good and very cheap for laying over uneven floorboards before you tile or pour self-levelling compound (see fake flagstone floor, page 130). And let's not forget, it's also dead easy to cut.

MDF – Medium Density Fibreboard is by far the most versatile of the lot. There are no words to describe just how useful MDF is, but if you come across two consecutive projects in this book that don't feature it, then some of the pages must be stuck together. There has been a lot of debate recently on the health risks associated with certain chemicals in MDF. Some of the points are absolutely valid, some are scaremongering. As with most things in life, it's simply a question of common sense. If you're going to cut up material that makes a lot of dust, do it outside and wear a mask.

A full sheet of MDF is 2.4x1.2m (8x4ft) and most smaller sheets tend to be easy divisions of this. If your timber supplier does cutting to order, he's likely to have some odd-shaped offcuts knocking about, which are usually cheaper than the standard sizes and may be just what you need for the particular job in hand. Note that MDF comes in various thicknesses, but needs regular support to make it stand up to heavy load-bearing duties.

PLASTERBOARD – While you wouldn't normally be working with this material, you will come up against it fairly regularly in the average home. Plasterboard is what they make interior walls and ceilings out of. It is made by sandwiching liquid plaster between layers of paper and then letting the whole thing go rock solid. The finished boards are then just nailed on to either side of wooden studs to form the cavity walls that split your

flat or house up into rooms. To drill into it you'll need a masonry bit, and to secure anything to it you'll need some cavity wall plugs or fixings. Not wishing to blind you with science and technology, the easiest way to establish whether the wall you are fixing to is solid or cavity is to tap it with your knuckles. If it sounds hollow, it is; if it doesn't, it's not.

PLYWOOD – More expensive than other manufactured boards, plywood is actually a sandwich of thin wood slices glued together so that the grains run in opposite directions. In the size to strength ratio stakes, it takes a lot

of beating. Three-ply is suitable for small shelves; seven-ply will build you a tank. Because it's made of real wood veneers plywood should be your choice where you need the convenience of board with the look of timber.

VENEER BOARDS – If you want the look of a hardwood without the guilt, there are several veneer boards on the market. Essentially these have a softwood or fibre core with a thin skin of hardwood all around the outside. They look like expensive timber, but they have the constructional limitations of your average fibreboard.

From bottom left to top right: chipboard, MDF, hardboard and plywood.

the three 'Fs'

Now far be it from me to make my job seem easy, but you really don't have to be a master craftsman to revamp your radiators or transform your tables. You just need some basic tools and materials and some basic common sense. There are three stages to any project, and they all begin with F...

FABRICATING

Unless you have decided to whittle a scale model of the Eiffel Tower from an old tree trunk, there are very few DIY projects that come in one piece. Everything that's going to be fitted together in the finished article will need to be fabricated (made) first, and if it's going to fit together properly it needs to be fabricated correctly. This is where every project starts and where many of them very nearly finish. Get this bit right and the rest of your day will be a dream.

MEASURING – There's an old saying that goes 'the bigger the project, the bigger the margin for error'. In fact it's such an old saying that the last time anyone used it was when they were building the tower

at Pisa. Good workmanship is about precision. I'm not talking about 'precise to the nearest half inch', I'm talking about precise to the nearest eighth of an inch, I'm talking about precise to the width of a saw blade. When you measure something, make sure you do it with a decent rule – not a bit of string, not a dressmaker's cloth tape and not a stick with pencil marks on it! Once you have measured something, measure it again and then write the measurements down somewhere. You have endless opportunities to use a rule, but you get only one chance to cut or drill something.

MARKING – All the accurate measuring in the world is not going to help if you then mark things up with your kid's felt pens. Use a sharp pencil to draw your cut lines and a sharp point to mark your drilling points. Even the width of a pencil line is going to have an effect on the accuracy of intricate projects, so work out whether you should be sawing right down the middle of your cut line or down one side of it. Finally, don't

rush. If you rush something, you're far more likely to mess up. You'll be marking up for only a few minutes, but you'll be living with the end results for a lot longer than that.

Use a decent rule, a thin pencil line and an accurate spirit level to ensure that everything is straight.

CUTTING – If you're using a large handsaw, make sure you've got the right one for the job. There are saws specifically designed to cut across the grain of the wood, along the grain of the wood and through manufactured boards. Lay your index finger along the side of the handle as you cut: this will keep the blade straight and true. Smaller joints just need a short tenon saw, which

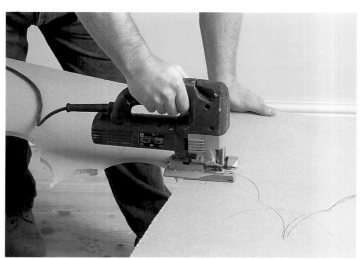

Keep your index finger on the saw and your saw on the marked line for accurate cuts.

has a rigid spine to keep the blade from bending. You can get special tools to keep your saws sharp (saw-setting pliers and saw sharpeners), or you might even find your local hardware store can sharpen tools for you. Electrically powered circular saws or jigsaws are far quicker and easier to use than manual ones, but make sure you have the right blade fitted for the material you are working with and that the blade is in good condition. All material needs to be well supported when you cut, especially when you come to the last little bit: if something's going to rip or tear, that's when it will happen.

Make sure your work is well supported when you cut.

DRILLING – Nothing to it, right? Wrong. There is one way to get drilling right but endless alternatives to mess it up. First off, make sure you have the right drill bit for the material you are drilling into. You can get different drills for wood, masonry, metal and even tiles. They're all clearly marked up on the packet, but what happens when you've lost the packet? Familiarize yourself with what the tips look like so that you don't end up blunting a perfectly good drill bit in completely the wrong material. Second, pick the right size bit. Screws, plugs and drill bits are all marked up with the same system of sizes. A hole drilled into the wall needs to be the same size as the plug you are going to fit into it. A pilot hole drilled into wood needs to be smaller than the screw it's intended for. Third, don't drill holes deeper than they need to be. A piece of brightly coloured electrical tape stuck around the drill bit is a quick way of checking how far in you have gone (see the *Plug/Screw* technique, page 28). Finally, when you drill, hold the material you are working with so that it can't move about, and drill into it at a right angle. Any screw will follow the line of the hole it's going into and if the hole is at an angle, then everything else will be too.

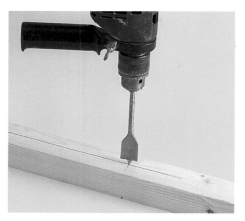

Drill at right angles to the material for accurate holes.

FIXING

You've made all the parts, now you just need to get them to stay together. Fear not, there is a dizzying array of fixings available to you to ensure that your precious pieces stay mated for life. Always get a few more of what you need while you're down at the shops. That way you'll build up a collection of fixings that can be adapted to most situations you'll have to cope with.

CORRUGATED FASTENERS – Specialist fixings, usually employed to hold together butt joints (see page 30), these have a much higher resistance to being pulled apart and are quicker to drive in than the usual screws.

LOST HEAD NAILS and **PANEL PINS** – Perfect for securing strips of architrave or beading that you have glued on to other timber (see tongue-and-groove wall panelling, page 40). It's also a neat trick to blunt the points before you hammer them in, so that they don't split thin strips of wood. You're unlikely to need anything other than 25mm (1in) panel pins and 50mm (2in) lost heads. A pin hammer will be fine to drive in the panel pins, but you'll need something with a bit more weight if you want to drive lost head nails into your walls.

MASONRY NAILS and **WIRE NAILS** – Larger than panel pins and lost head nails, these will cope with holding together much bigger sheets of material while your glue is drying.

NAILS – Contrary to popular belief, nails are not God's gift to the world of fixings and do not possess the superhuman power of being able to weld together permanently any two materials you can name, including Kryptonite. Nails are very useful where they're suitable and a liability where they're not. If you want to hold things together while they glue, nails are great. If you want to hold things together to stop them sliding sideways, nails are fine. If you want to hold things together to stop them pulling apart, nails are going to be a sad disappointment to you. Bright nails (below) will be suitable for most indoor projects you will want to tackle if you don't mind seeing the heads of the nails.

PLASTERBOARD NAILS – These are deliberately harder to pull out, but must still be used at regular intervals to create a secure fixing.

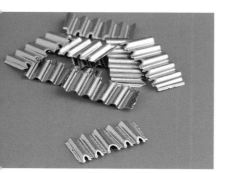

Corrugated fasteners

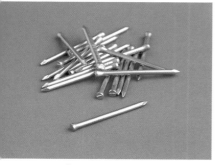

Panel pins

Lost head nails

Masonry nails

Bright nails

SCREWS – Now we're talking. Screws are nails with attitude, and teeth. If you want to do a job properly, these are the boys you need. They come in two main types, slot-head and cross-head, each requiring a different type of screwdriver to get them in. If there's a choice, I'd always go for the cross-head variety, which are less prone to letting the screwdriver slip off and can still be worked from some pretty hairy angles. If you want your screws to disappear flush with the wood for painting over, get the everyday steel flat-head type. However, if you want to leave the screw heads proud, as part of the finished work, you can get domed heads, which also look really nice in black or brass.

Most screws are designed for worming their way into both plastic wall plugs (see plugs, page 24) or timber, but if you're working with materials such as plasterboard or chipboard, you'll need special screws to do it right. Screws come in loads of different lengths and thicknesses.

Always drill thin pilot holes for your screws to make sure they go in smoothly and accurately. If you are working with brass screws, these can actually break if you force them too much, so drive a steel screw into your pilot hole first to pave the way. Steel screws are designed so that the thread goes right up to the head for maximum grip and are not tapered in any way, so there's less chance of anything splitting as they go in. They're actually meant for plasterboard, but they're also perfect for MDF.

The only widths of screw you are ever likely to need are sizes 6, 8 and 10. To be honest, size 8 will get you through just about everything in this book. The length of screw you require is dependent on the project in hand, but the ground rules are these. If you are screwing timber into wall plugs, your screws need to be just less than the combined depth of both batten and plug. If you are securing timber to timber (or board to board), your screws need to be about twice the depth of the thinnest piece of material. Cross-head screws will give you the best grip, so make sure you have a screwdriver that will fit them and then avoid all contact with the slot-head variety whenever possible.

TACKS – Used to hold lightweight board or fabric in place, but you need a lot of them to keep everything firm.

Tacks

Plasterboard screws

Domed head nails

Plasterboard nails   Slot-head nails

Cross-head nails

PLUGS – If you're attaching something to masonry or plasterboard, you're going to need a plug. These little tubes of plastic are pressed into holes drilled in the wall and provide something soft for the screws to get their teeth into. There are two varieties available, depending on the type of surface you want them for. Solid wall plugs are straight or slightly tapered, with little serrations down the sides. These are what you need when you're screwing into bricks or concrete. Cavity wall plugs are for plasterboard walls or ceilings. They have little 'arms' on either side, which splay out behind the plasterboard as you tighten the screw. For more demanding cavity wall jobs (where the load-bearing is significant), there is a whole range of elaborate metal fixings that you can choose from. Most recently available are 'self-drill' plasterboard fixings, which are a cross between a wall plug and a screw. You twist them into a small pilot hole with a screwdriver and then treat them like a conventional plug. Quick and easy to fit, they work a treat.

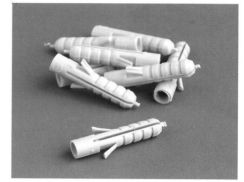

Solid wall plugs

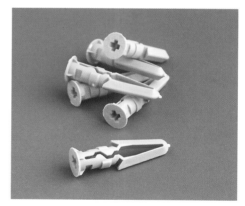

Cavity wall plugs

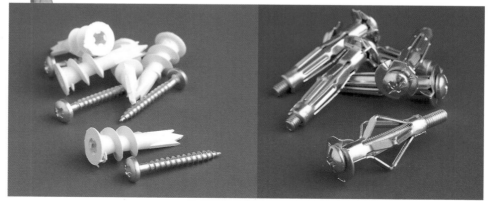

Self-drill plasterboard fixings

Heavy-duty plasterboard fixings

GLUE – It would be pointless me trying to tell you here exactly which glues you should be using for which jobs. It seems they can always invent new ones faster than I can type. However, the basic rules are these. A good wood glue gives a fantastically strong join in timber, but don't always believe the drying times stated on the tube. Leave your work for 24 hours before you put any real stress on it. If you're glueing wood to the wall, use a panel adhesive. Most of these are pretty innocuous, but if you get one that smells at all potent, make sure you work with the windows open. Finally, no glue is designed to work with dirt. Always make sure your surfaces are absolutely clean and dry before you spread on the adhesive, then wipe off the excess before it dries.

HINGES – For such a simple-looking piece of pivoting metal, the hinge has caused more aggravation in my life than anything else. Putting these things on so that your doors swing properly is actually extremely difficult, so the only two hinges I ever tend to use are the easiest of all to fit. Funny that. For your average, everyday hinge duties I would always go for something called 'flush hinges'. These things don't need any complicated recesses cut to accommodate them in the wood, so installation is as easy as it's ever going to get. For cupboard and wardrobe doors, go for 'concealed adjustable hinges'. These are the type you usually find inside your kitchen cupboard doors. The major advantage they have is that even after you've fixed them into place, you can still use the little screw adjustments they feature to make sure your doors are straight and level. Better still, most are spring loaded to hold your doors tightly closed when shut.

Concealed adjustable hinges

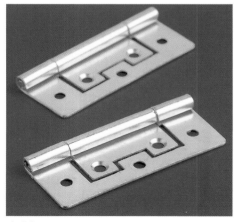

Panel adhesive (top) and wood glue (bottom)

Flush hinges

FIXING TECHNIQUES

All the way through this book I talk about three types of combination fixing techniques: *Glue/Nail*, *Glue/Screw* and *Plug/Screw*. You won't be surprised to hear that they are no more complicated than they sound. I'm a great believer in making things that last, which means putting them together properly in the first place. Follow these simple steps each time and your works of art will last far longer than you ever dreamed.

GLUE/NAIL – Make sure all the bits you are about to connect are the right size and the right fit, then smear on enough adhesive to spread out across the join, but not so much that it spreads out across the carpet. Press the pieces into place and hammer in small panel pins or slightly larger lost head nails to secure everything while the glue dries. If you have big fingers and find inserting little panel pins too fiddly, try pressing the pin point into a thin piece of card to hold the pin upright before the first hammer tap. Also, there is a special tool called a nail punch which you can use to drive the nail heads just below the surface without bruising the wood with over-enthusiastic hammer blows.

Remember, the success of your join is dependent on the glue, not the nails. Make sure you have used plenty of adhesive and then only put in enough fixings to hold the

Nails are not very attractive, so use them sparingly.

timber firmly together while the glue dries. If you want to finish the job properly then you are going to have to fill and paint all the holes your nail heads have left behind so some over-eager hammering at this stage will be counter-productive later on.

GLUE/SCREW – Place your timber in position (holding it with clamps if necessary) and use a thin drill bit to make tiny pilot holes in both pieces of wood to be joined. Mark the

timber with a couple of pencil lines to make sure you can line the holes up again before you apply the glue. Once the pieces are glued and pressed together again, drive in a correctly sized screw through each pilot hole. With softwood it's pretty easy to get the flat-head screws flush with the surface just by using an ordinary screwdriver. If you're using a power screwdriver, you'll have your work cut out trying not to lose the screw altogether!

HANDY ANDY'S HOT TIPS

Instead of positioning, marking and repositioning your glue-covered materials, you can save a lot of time and effort by doing the whole thing in one go. Make sure all the elements will fit properly, then apply your adhesive and clamp everything together. Drill your pilot holes and drive in your screws while the clamps are keeping things rigid. As soon as the screws are in you can release the clamps and carry on working as if the glue were already dry.

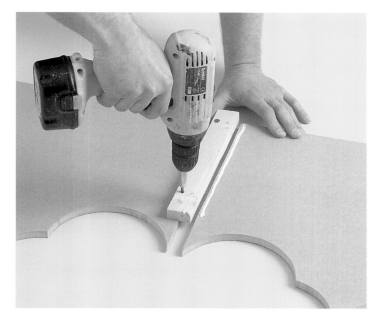

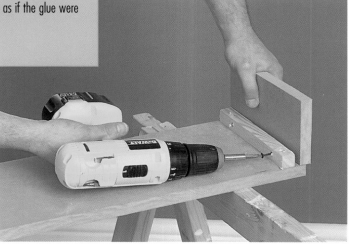

Drilling pilot holes is the only way to ensure your screws will go in without complication, but make sure you keep the materials lined up accurately between drilling the pilot holes and driving in the screws themselves.

PLUG/SCREW – Unless you are a claustrophobic architect it seems likely that walls are going to feature quite prominently in your home. Fixings things to those walls means using the *Plug/Screw* technique and if you don't want to spend the rest of your life with free-standing furniture, you'd better get the hang of it now...

1 If you are fixing a batten to a wall or ceiling, hold the timber securely and then drill some thin pilot holes all the way through it where you want each screw to be. Now, use a spirit level to hold the timber accurately in place on the wall or ceiling.

HANDY ANDY'S HOT TIPS

Drilling into walls is always a bit of an adventure, but there are a few ways to avoid too much excitement. Always use the right drill bit; usually a masonry bit, but a ceramic capable one if you're drilling through tiles. Don't drill deeper than the wall plug you are using and don't go drilling next to any light switches or electrical sockets. Some of the stuff inside the solid walls of your house is amazingly tough going, if you're not making any progress with a particular hole then get a drill with hammer action, they get through anything.

2 Use your bradawl to mark drilling points through the pilot holes and then take the timber away.

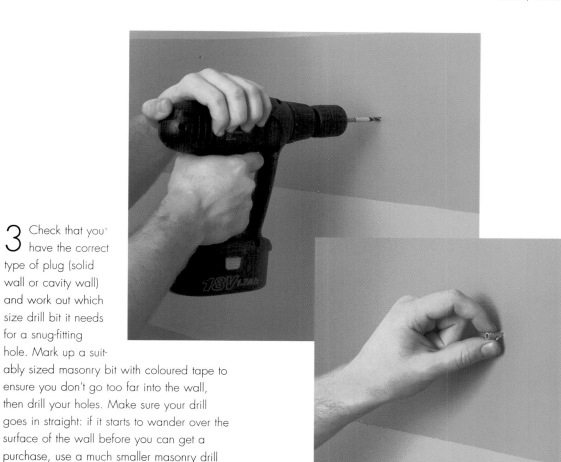

3 Check that you have the correct type of plug (solid wall or cavity wall) and work out which size drill bit it needs for a snug-fitting hole. Mark up a suitably sized masonry bit with coloured tape to ensure you don't go too far into the wall, then drill your holes. Make sure your drill goes in straight: if it starts to wander over the surface of the wall before you can get a purchase, use a much smaller masonry drill bit to bore a pilot hole first.

4 Blow the dust out of each hole and tap in your plugs. They should be a nice tight fit and sit exactly flush with the surface of the wall.

5 You can start each screw a little way into the pilot holes in the timber before you put the batten up into position and then drive the screw fully home into the plug when it's in place. Again, try to get your screw heads flush with the timber so that they don't leave a mark when you paint.

JOINTS – Once you get into the joys of working with wood, you will quickly realize that there are all manner of carpentry techniques available to you to make your projects a lot stronger to live with and a lot more attractive to look at. The first and most important place you can aim to make these improvements is wherever two bits of wood need joining. A lasting and professional looking join between two bits of wood comes down to three elements: how much surface there is for the glue to adhere to; how much one piece of wood is enclosed by the other; and how accurate you have been with all your cuts. For making all the examples listed below, your best friends are a set square (or sliding bevel), a tenon saw and the humble pencil.

BUTT JOINT – Dead simple and very quick, but not particularly fancy. Here the wood is simply glued surface to surface and secured by nails or screws. It's not really that strong a join and is best used where you won't have to look at it all day. If necessary, you can always use a corrugated fastener or even a couple of screws to make this join a bit stronger, but even then don't rely on it for heavy duties.

MITRE JOINT – So long as you've bought or made yourself a mitre block (see page 15), this is an easy way to get a nice-looking join where wood meets wood at a corner. It's the standard join around picture frames and can be strengthened by a nail or screw driven into one side (see timber pot rack, page 150). To make life even easier, they now make things called 'mitre clamps' that will hold the joint exactly in position while your

Butt joint

Mitre joint

glue sets. Mitres are both stronger and more attractive than the humble butt joint.

HALVING JOINT – More fancy, more fun. These joints are great for securing structures made of 50x25mm (2x1in) wood or similar. Each piece to be joined has one half of the timber cut away where they meet so that everything fits perfectly flush when you press them together. A spot of glue and a securing screw and you have a very strong joint indeed. If you want to get very fancy, you can even experiment with making the cuts wedge-shaped, and before you know it you'll have a dovetail joint. Flash or what?

MORTISE AND TENON JOINT – Less of a joint and more of a national institution, the mortise and tenon technique is one of the oldest and strongest tricks around. Basically it's just a slot (or mortise) in one piece of wood that accepts a smaller protrusion (tenon) sticking

out of the other, and if you don't do it carefully, that's exactly what it will look like as well! This joint really needs some time and care lavished upon it and must be very accurately constructed to work properly. The slot is best made by first drilling a series of large holes side by side and then using a chisel to square everything off. The tenon is simply made by marking up your timber with carefully measured lines and then cutting off what you don't want with a tenon saw. Believe me, once you've glued something together with a well-made mortise and tenon joint, it won't be going anywhere for a long, long time. This technique was used to hold together massive houses and huge boats long before anyone came along with screws and adhesives, so if you can't eventually make a little bit of furniture with all the help you have today, I'm taking up welding. This joint works equally well in the middle of a batten as it does at the end of one.

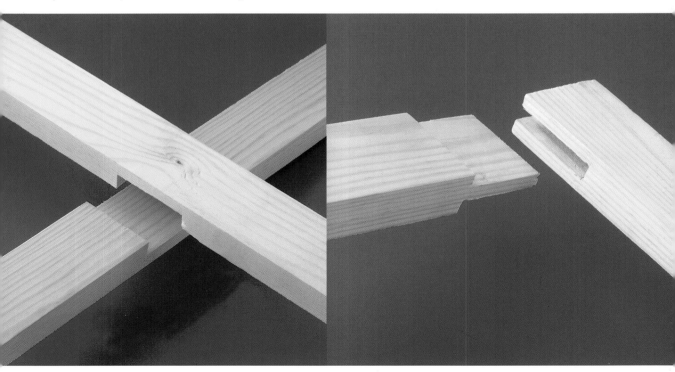

Halving joint   Mortise and tenon joint

FINISHING

If you think you're done, you're not. No matter how brilliant and inspired your carpentry skills have become, and no matter how sophisticated your construction techniques, if you don't take the time to finish your projects correctly, they'll never look right. A good finish to your work is not just about making it look better: proper care for the wood at this stage will protect it from dirt, damage and the ravages of heat and light. A smooth, sealed surface is also a lot easier to clean. But don't panic, it's not as complicated as it sounds. For most of the projects in this book the only thing you'll need to worry about once the fabricating and fixing are taken care of is a little filling and sanding.

FILLING AND SANDING – Surfaces that are going to be painted need to be flat and smooth: a lick of paint will hide a multitude of sins, but it won't hide holes and cracks. Press some wood filler into all the nail and screwhead holes you left behind, and use some more to cover up any gaps in your joints, not that there'll be any of course! Wait until the filler's dry, then rub everything down with sandpaper. If there are lots of lumps and bumps, use rough sandpaper across the grain first, then finish off with finer paper along the grain. If it needs more help than that, a hand- or electric-powered plane will give you a perfect surface in minutes. Blow off all the dust and you're done.

OIL AND VARNISH – For surfaces such as table-tops or kitchen counters, where you want to keep the original wood on show, there are various products available to protect your timber without sealing it away from view. Something like Danish Oil, or a wax equivalent, can be rubbed in with a soft rag. Top it up with a new coat every few weeks and it will eventually start to improve the colour and the feel of the wood itself. If you want a more permanent protection for your handi-work, check out the new acrylic varnishes which are now available. Water-based for ease of use, these are still formulated to create a hard, impermeable layer over the timber to keep out the muck and the mois-ture. Better for the environment to boot.

When planing (above) and sanding (right) clamp the material tightly to prevent it slipping.

Bottom left to top right: colour-washed walls; a dresser aged by wiping wax over a flat paint colour; a chest of drawers is given a gothic look with silver aerosol paint and decoupage .

PAINTING AND PAINT EFFECTS – Once your surface is sanded smooth, there are still a few things to attend to if you want to make a perfect job of painting it. Knot holes in new wood can leak sap through fresh paint, so dab them down with knotting compound before you start. For a truly luminous finish to your paint, treat the wood to a coat of primer first. Use the right product for the right type of wood and this will also help seal the timber. The best news of all is that there are now some excellent water-based paints on the market especially designed for woodwork. The smell doesn't hang around the house for ages, and you can wash your brushes out under the tap.

If you're painting MDF, you are in for a treat. This material takes a flat colour beautifully and you only need to prime it if you want a particularly bright or delicate finish. Use a paint roller for large areas and touch in the edges with a small brush. However, flat colours tend to be few and far between on *Changing Rooms,* and despite the fact that paint effects are not really my bag, it's impossible to work on the programme without picking up the gist of all that 'designer speak'…

Colour washing – Basically, this is a flat coat of colour with a lighter shade brushed over the top. The second coat needs to be diluted in ratios ranging from half paint, half water up to one part paint and nine parts water. The more dilute the top coat, the more you'll see of the base colour and the more 'washy' the end result will be.

Distressing – A paint technique rather than an opinion, distressing is used to make your brand new projects look like they've been there for years. All you have to do is rub a bit of candle or furniture wax over your first coat of colour once it's dry. Do this in a very patchy style. Now, paint a second colour over everything and let that dry also. Finally, use some fine sandpaper or even a cloth to rub away the areas of wax. You'll be left with an effect where your base colour seems to break through the top coat just like old paint peeling away after years of neglect. The designers usually put pale colours over dark colours when they use this technique.

STAINS – Less popular than they once were, wood stains can do anything from enhancing to obliterating the natural finish of timber. There are a number of types available, but I prefer the water-based ones. Designed to bring out the natural grain of your wood rather than disguise it, water-based stains take longer to apply and longer to take effect but the end results are well worth the extra trouble. Be prepared to rub down the surface with fine sandpaper between coats.

BEDROOMS

I've always thought that if you're going to embark upon a strange new habit, the best place to start is in the privacy of your own bedroom, and DIY is no exception. There are two very compelling reasons why sleeping quarters are always a great destination for the early fruits of your homebuild handiwork. If the project turns out a dream, it'll be there to delight and inspire you last thing at night and first thing in the morning. If it turns out a nightmare, you're the only one who has to go up there, and that's only when it's dark.

beaded radiator cover

The thing about radiators is that they always feel brilliant when you're pressed up against them, but they can look a dreadful eyesore when you stand back. Here's a trick to keep the heat, but lose the headache. A radiator cover will not only hide the plumbing, it will also give you a useful shelf into the bargain.

MATERIALS & EQUIPMENT

Tape measure
Pencil
Handsaw or jigsaw with timber-cutting blade
5x2.5cm (2x1in) timber batten (twice the length of your radiator)
Spirit level
Drill with 6mm masonry bit and 3mm wood bit for pilot holes
Bradawl
6mm wall plugs (solid or cavity)
Screwdriver or screwdriver bit for drill
4.5cm (1¾in) size 8 wood screws
About 1.2x1.2m (4x4ft) of 2cm (¾in) MDF or ply
Wood glue
10mm wood bit to get jigsaw started

Radiators can be the hardest things to incorporate into a room's decorative scheme. A cover will give you far more scope to turn those slabs of metal into something you can really be proud of.

1 Measure and cut two timber battens to match the width of the radiator you want to hide. *Plug/Screw* one batten to the wall, ensuring that the top of it is at least 5cm (2in) above the top of the radiator, so that the hot air can still circulate when you're done. Use a spirit level to ensure that the batten is straight on the wall.

2 Screw the second batten to the floor so that its front edge is at least 2.5cm (1in) forward of the radiator. This cover doesn't want to be too snug or you'll just end up heating the MDF and not the room.

HANDY ANDY'S HOT TIPS

The *Changing Rooms* designer Linda Barker made the beaded decorations in the radiatior cover by alternately threading painted beads and home-made paper tubes on lengths of string, which are then hung just short of the floor. The tubes were made by wetting 20cm (8in) squares of paper with PVA glue and then wrapping them around drinking straws to form the shape. A quick way to paint your beads is by shaking them about in a plastic bag which already has some emulsion paint poured into it.

The design of your radiator cover can be as ornate as you like. Lengths of rope can be substituted for the beads and paper tubes hung between the MDF panels.

3 Measure and cut a shelf out of 1.25cm (½in) MDF the exact width and depth of your planned radiator cover, then *Glue/Screw* it to the top of the wall batten.

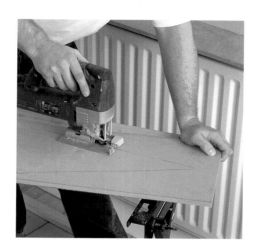

4 Decide on the size of gap you would like between the front panels, then cut three pieces of 2cm (¾in) MDF for the panels themselves. Heightwise, they need to fit exactly into the space between the floor and the underside of your shelf. Now mark out (see page 20) and remove a decorative shape from the centre of each panel. (Make sure each shape is identical across the three panels to avoid later ridicule.) To start off the jigsaw cut, drill a hole inside the area of MDF that will be removed and use this to get the blade in.

5 *Glue/Screw* your front panels to the underside of the shelf and the front of the floor batten, making sure they are evenly spaced across the radiator. Linda, the designer, used strings of painted beads hung from the shelf to fill in the four gaps across the front. We also painted both radiator and finished cover the same colour to complete the effect.

If your creative juices are at the high-water mark, there are many other ways this cover can be decorated. Try using some short lengths of thin metal piping instead of the beads, or what about some sheets of metal mesh pinned to the back of the MDF panels? It's all waiting for you down at the local DIY store...

BRIGHT IDEAS

You don't have to stick to the layout I've shown you here. If you have a particularly large radiator, you can use more than three panels to divide up the space, and the shapes you cut out of each can be as elaborate as your jigsawing skills will allow. You can even have more than one shape in each panel if you like.

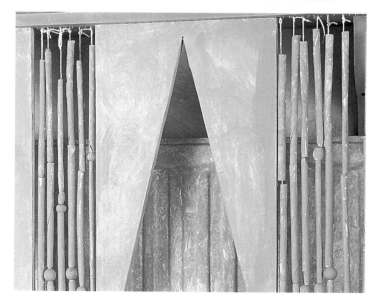

tongue-and-groove wall panelling

If you think walls are only for painting, papering or climbing, you're in for a pleasant surprise. Here's a great idea for adding instant class to almost any room – tongue-and-groove panelling with no tongue-and-groove timber!

I've opted for a simple V-shaped groove in these panels, which gives a classic elegance to the room, but there are many other, more elaborate router bits available if you want to walk a little on the wild side.

MATERIALS & EQUIPMENT

Tape measure
Pencil
Timber straight edge
1.25cm (½in) MDF or ply (length according to the size of your room)
Handsaw or jigsaw with timber-cutting blade
Router with V-profile bit
Panel adhesive
Claw hammer
4cm (1½in) lost head nails
Nail punch
5x2.5cm (2x1in) planed timber (according to the size of your room)
5cm (2in) architrave (according to the size of your room)
4cm (1½in) panel pins
Drill with 3mm wood bit for pilot holes
4.5cm (1¾in) size 8 wood screws
Wood filler

1 Decide on the height you require for your wall panelling and cut MDF panels to fit around the entire room. You're going to create grooves in the panels about 15cm (6in) apart, and marking up the cut lines is the most crucial part of this whole project. It's probably best to lay all your panels out in order so that you can measure the positions for each groove as one continuous effect. You can use a piece of timber to mark out the lines, but make sure it's got a nice straight edge before you do so.

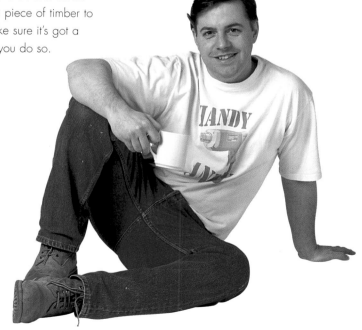

BRIGHT IDEAS

Make sure you hide any holes left by the nail heads with a bit of wood filler, then paint the whole thing to finish it off. Different colours for the panelling and shelving looks very effective and you can also glue and pin a little strip of shaped beading (decorative wooden edging) along the front of the shelf to make it look really smart.

Below: Close-up of V-profile bit

2 Use your straight edge timber again as a guide for the router. You'll need a V-profile bit for the grooves and they should be cut in no more than half the depth of the MDF. Make sure you've got your straight edge and your router set correctly before cutting each and every groove. One mistake and that's the whole sheet of MDF ruined.

HANDY ANDY'S HOT TIPS

A router does two impressive-looking jobs very efficiently. It will either shape the edges of your material to give it a decorative effect, or it will cut different shaped grooves into flat material for aesthetic or construction reasons. It can only do this job if it has a secure edge to run against as it travels. Some routers have a sliding guard which can be set to run along the edge of board or timber. Where this is not possible, you should always use clamps to secure a straight edge in place or to act as a guide. You should always use clamps to secure a straight edge in place and use this as a firm guide along which to slide the router as you work.

3 To fix the MDF to the walls, squirt plenty of panel adhesive on to each panel, press the panel on to the wall and secure in place with a few lost head nails.

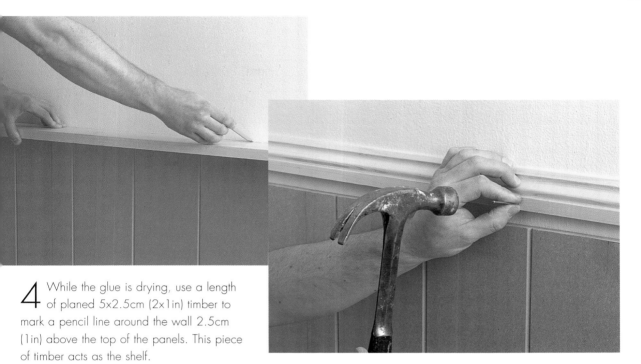

4 While the glue is drying, use a length of planed 5x2.5cm (2x1in) timber to mark a pencil line around the wall 2.5cm (1in) above the top of the panels. This piece of timber acts as the shelf.

5 Use more panel adhesive to glue a run of architrave all around the walls, then pin in place with panel pins to secure. Make sure the underside of the architrave is exactly level with the line you've just marked, or the shelf won't fit back in.

6 Use panel adhesive and screws to secure the planed timber shelf back into the gap. Screw up into the architrave from underneath and no one will notice how it's been fixed.

copper pipe curtain rail

Curtain poles are just for holding up curtains, right? Wrong. With a little bit of imagination your curtain poles can be as much a design feature of a room as the fabric hanging from them. All you need to create the clever idea described here is a bit of old copper pipe and a couple of wardrobe rail brackets. You can use the new rail to replace existing curtain fixtures or to conjure up some eye-cataching wizardry on a bland old window.

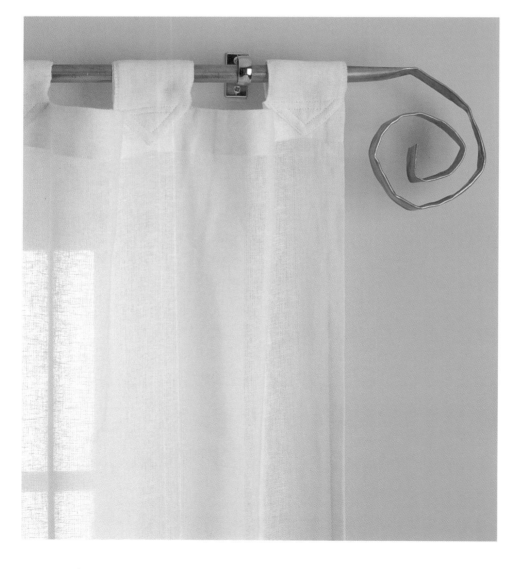

Once you've got the hang of bending the pipe ends and realized just how flexible copper can be, why not have a go at zigzags or candy-twist spirals? There's plenty more pipe where that came from if it doesn't work out.

1 Measure and cut a length of copper pipe so that it is about 46cm (18in) wider than the window frame. Copper pipe can be cut with a hacksaw, but it is a far neater process if you use a specially designed pipe-cutter for the job. They're pretty cheap and readily available at all the DIY stores. All you do to operate them is gently tighten the cutting wheel on to your pipe and keep turning and tightening the device until you're through.

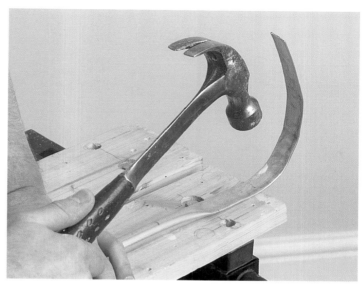

2 If your rail brackets are a tight fit around the copper pipe, make sure you thread them on before you flatten the ends. Lay the pipe on a hard surface and use a hammer to beat flat about 20cm (8in) at either end.

MATERIALS & EQUIPMENT

Tape measure
Pencil
Hacksaw or pipe-cutting tool
2cm (¾in) copper pipe (about 46cm (18in)
  longer than the width of your window)
Hammer
Large pliers
2 or 3 wardrobe rail brackets
Curtain rings (if needed)
6mm wall plugs
Screwdriver or screwdriver bit for drill
2cm (¾in) size 8 wood screws (if not supplied
  with rail brackets)
Drill with 6mm masonry bit
Spirit level with timber straight edge

3 Now use some pliers or the handle of the hammer to bend the flattened pipe into a spiralling curl at each end. Start by bending the end of the pipe and then work your way along in an ever-looser curve. Don't worry about getting it into a perfect spiral, this is art!

5 You can still bend the copper into its final shape after the pole is up, just to get everything looking perfect.

The days of hiding curtain fixings with pelmets are long gone. There's nothing like a bold curtain pole design for setting off your window.

4 *Plug/Screw* two rail brackets to the wall about 15cm (6in) above the window. Make sure they are level with each other when you fix them, unless you really want to have all your curtains down one end of the pole. When fixing things like wardrobe rail brackets to the wall, you will need short screws: ones about the same length as your wall plugs will be fine, and these are often supplied with the brackets themselves.

BRIGHT IDEAS

The shapes at each end of the pole can be as ornate as you want, but make sure you allow enough copper pipe to create them when you first cut the pipe to length.

copper pipe bed curtain rail

Here's a neat idea: a four-poster bed with no posts, and all for the price of some bits of plumber's copper pipe. This project is particularly suited to rooms with high ceilings, where there is plenty of space to create a dramatic drop of curtain material at each corner of the bed. The end result not only looks elegant and timeless, but will also seem to draw down the space above you and create a room of more intimate and more pleasing proportions.

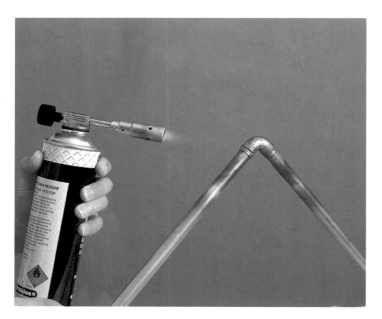

MATERIALS & EQUIPMENT

Tape measure
Pencil
2cm (¾in) copper pipe (according to the size
   of your bed)
4 x 2cm (¾in) copper elbow joints
Hacksaw or pipe-cutting tool
Epoxy resin glue or solder and blowlamp
4 wardrobe rail brackets
Curtain rings (if needed)
Drill with 6mm masonry bit for pilot holes
Plasterboard fixing plugs (one for each screw
   hole in your rail brackets)
Screwdriver or screwdriver bit for drill
2cm (¾in) size 8 wood screws (if not supplied
   with rail brackets)

1 Measure the length of the sides, top and bottom of your bed. Cut out lengths of copper pipe to match these measurements. Using these lengths of copper pipes and 90° elbow joints, glue or solder together a rectangular frame the same size as your bed. Don't forget to thread on four wardrobe rail brackets and your curtain rings before you secure the last corner. That would be particularly embarrassing.

This simple construction technique doesn't just have to apply to your bedroom. You could adapt the project to create a shower cubicle curtain, or even use the same idea above your bath.

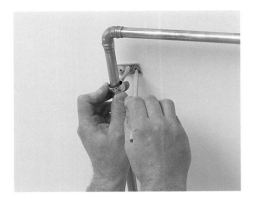

2 Hold the frame up against your ceiling, directly over the bed, and mark drill-hole positions for the rail brackets in each corner. Make sure the brackets are in the same position at each corner, otherwise it will look very odd when you're finished. If you can manage this without any help, you are either an octopus or a circus performer.

3 Drill your marked holes and insert cavity wall plugs or self-drill plasterboard fixings, which are both specially designed for use in plasterboard. If you get much resistance from the drill, it simply means that you've hit one of the ceiling joists above, so you can use a conventional wood screw to complete the task.

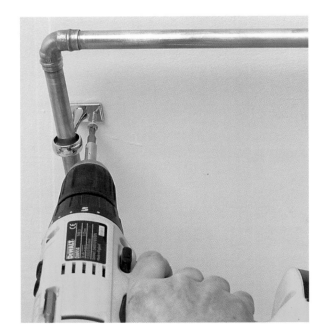

BRIGHT IDEAS

As an alternative to the method described here, you can always secure two of your rail brackets to the wall instead of the ceiling, or you can even use metal wires to suspend the curtain rail from secure fixing points hidden up in the loft.

4 Plug/Screw your rail brackets into place, hang your curtains, and stand back to admire. Plasterboard fixings are pretty robust, but your curtains are not really designed for swinging from. Please conduct your normal bedroom activities with this in mind. We'll say no more about it.

The curtain rail can either be fixed directly to the walls and ceiling (above), or suspended on wires where you have enough height (below).

HANDY ANDY'S HOT TIPS

There are three different ways that you can join copper pipes together for a project like this. Soldering on elbow joints is the normal way and it's easier than you might imagine. The trick is to piece the pipes for each join together and then heat the metal with a blowtorch; after a few seconds it will be hot enough to melt the solder when you touch it in place. You'll find that the molten solder will be drawn into the elbow joint, where it will harden as soon as it cools. If you don't fancy that, you can always buy 'compression' joints which look a little more bulky, but can be fitted with just a couple of spanners. Finally, you could just glue the joints together with a strong epoxy resin, such as Araldite.

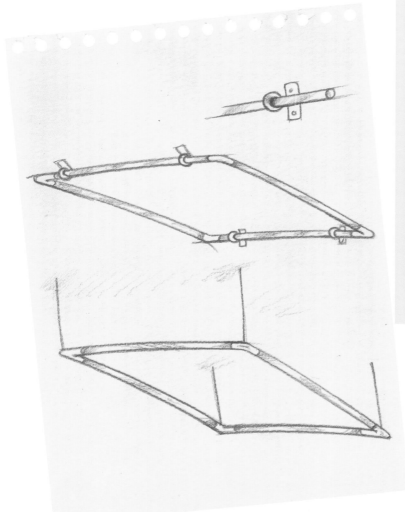

ornamental curtain pelmet

If you've got a lot of space, and a lot of stuff to hide, here's a project that will close off part of any room and provide a great design feature into the bargain. The way we live today puts pressure on the furniture in our home to serve several functions. Sometimes you need a permanent screen, sometimes just a temporary measure that makes more flexible use of the space available. This combination of solid pelmet and moveable curtains is the ideal solution where your needs have outgrown the limitations of just four walls. You can take this project up to any size, just so long as you keep the design in proportion to your room.

MATERIALS & EQUIPMENT

Tape measure
Pencil
1.25cm (½in) MDF or ply, enough to span
   your room and drop 46cm (18in)
Jigsaw with timber-cutting edge
Paper for template
Drill with 6mm masonry bit and 3mm wood bit
   for pilot holes
Wood glue
5x2.5cm (2x1in) timber (for upright battens on
   back of pelmet)
Screwdriver or screwdriver bit for drill
3cm (1¼in) size 8 wood screws (for battens
   on back of pelmet)
2.5x2.5cm (1x1in) timber (for horizontal
   battens on back of pelmet)
Cavity wall plugs or plasterboard fixing plugs,
   one every 15cm (6in) of span
4.5cm (1¾in) size 8 wood screws (for
   attaching pelmet battens to ceiling)

1 Measure and cut panels of MDF deep enough to accommodate your intended design (our pelmet was about 46cm (18in) deep) and wide enough to span the width of your room. Use a paper template to create a full-size motif for the repeating pattern along the pelmet and then use it to trace around so that you create an evenly spaced design along the full length of MDF. Jigsaw out the final shape.

We originally designed this pelmet to create a curtained-off storage area at one end of a room. However, if you have a long reception room that you'd like to break up into smaller areas, you could install two pelmets back to back and combine them with a couple of free-standing screens for a fast and fabulous room divider.

2 *Glue/Screw* some lengths of 5x2.5cm (2x1in) timber batten on to the back of the MDF panels to join them into one complete pelmet. Confirm that this is going to fit the room span exactly before you carry on. It's always best to check…

3 *Glue/Screw* a 2.5x2.5cm (1x1in) timber batten all along the top edge of the pelmet and wait for this to dry.

BRIGHT IDEAS

If the pelmet is going to be the same colour as the ceiling or walls, you can paint it once it's up. If not, it's a good idea to paint it before you finally secure the thing in place.

4 Hold your finished pelmet up into place, then use a thin drill bit to simultaneously create pilot holes in the timber batten and marks for the plugs in the ceiling. You'll need to secure the pelmet at intervals of about 15cm (6in) to support the weight.

Remove the pelmet, drill the ceiling where it's marked and insert your cavity wall plugs or self-drill plasterboard fixings. Finally, screw through the battens into the ceiling to secure your pelmet in place. Your curtains can either be secured straight on to the back of the pelmet using curtain track, or on to a rail fixed behind.

You can completely transform the shape and size of any room with this curtain pelmet project and you can also use your MDF design and choice of fabric to transform the mood at the same time. If you don't want to produce a motif of your own, then find a shape you like in a book or magazine and copy it.

the weekend wardrobe

Tired of using your clothes to carpet your bedroom? Fed up with drawers so full they won't close? Sounds like you need a wardrobe, and I've got just the thing. Fast, fitted and fashionably simple; all you need is a spare corner in your bedroom. This simple storage solution will provide stylish new accommodation for heaps of homeless outfits, and some welcome cupboard space in which to finally lose those shoes.

MATERIALS & EQUIPMENT

Tape measure
Pencil
About 9m (30ft) of 5x2.5cm (2x1in) timber batten
Handsaw or jigsaw with timber-cutting blade
Drill with 6mm masonry bit and 3mm wood bit for pilot holes
Bradawl
6mm wall plugs (solid or cavity)
4.5cm (1¾in) size 8 wood screws
Screwdriver or screwdriver bit for drill
2cm (¾in) MDF or ply (two 2.4x1.2m (8x4ft) sheets of MDF should do it)
Wood glue
Hole-cutter bit
4 concealed adjustable hinges
Chisel

1 Measure and mark lines across the floor and ceiling in a corner of your room to create two identical rectangles the size of your intended wardrobe. Cut timber battens to match the length of these lines, then *Plug/Screw* them to the floor and ceiling. The corners where the battens meet can be mitred or butt joined; let's face it, you're never going to see them again once the wardrobe's finished. *Plug/Screw* another timber batten up each wall to link up with the ends of the floor and ceiling battens.

Once you have mastered the art of instant wardrobes, why not take your skills elsewhere? This project will work equally well downstairs as a coats and shoes cupboard at the end of the hall, or even as a pots and pans storage area in a corner of the kitchen. Just add internal shelves to suit.

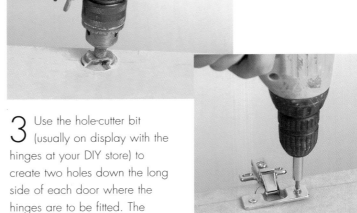

3 Use the hole-cutter bit (usually on display with the hinges at your DIY store) to create two holes down the long side of each door where the hinges are to be fitted. The hinges should be installed about 30cm (12in) from the top and bottom of the door.

4 Push one hinge into each of the four mounting holes and secure tightly in place with the specialist screws supplied.

2 Measure and cut two wardrobe doors and one side wall from MDF. Hold these panels in place to make sure that they fit correctly. Drill pilot holes around three sides of the side wall panel (about every 30 cm (12in)) and use these to *Glue/Screw* the MDF sheet to the floor, wall and ceiling battens. Make sure you drive your screws in far enough so that the heads end up flush with the surface of the MDF.

HANDY ANDY'S HOT TIPS

If you don't fancy the MDF handles used here, DIY stores have a huge range of ready-made styles with which you can finish off your wardrobe to perfection.

5 Use a chisel to prop the doors clear of the floor while you mark and then screw the hinges to the side walls. Once secure, you can tinker with the adjustable parts of these hinges to make sure your doors open and close with ease.

This wardrobe construction is designed to fit into an empty corner of your room and all the structural strength is supplied by the wall, floor and ceiling-mounted battens.

6 Finally, some offcuts of MDF can be put to good use as stylish handles for the doors. Two 15cm (6in) squares, with a smaller square behind each, can be glued and screwed in from the back at whatever height seems most comfortable for you to open the doors. Make sure your screws aren't too long, as sharp metal points sticking out of wardrobe door handles are never popular design features.

celebrity clothes-hangers

Get your morning off to a flying start, or scare the living daylights out of your family with these celebrity hangers. Quick, fun and easy to produce, you could use anyone you like…or hate. Try assorted politicians to turn your wardrobe into a 'cabinet', or an entire football team for that genuine 'locker-room' effect. Not only are these hangers great fun to create for your own wardrobe, they work even better as a bit of furnishing fun for the children. Scale the size down to match the shoulder width of your toddlers' togs and you might actually persuade the kids to hang something up for once in their lives.

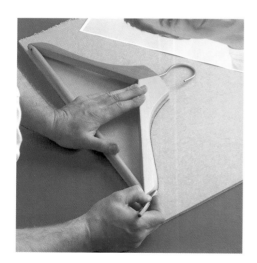

1 Trace around an ordinary coat-hanger on a piece of MDF. Photocopy your chosen illustration to the size you require.

2 Cut out the 'celebrity face', then position it on the MDF for tracing around. Cut out the whole finished shape with a jigsaw. (You'll need to drill a hole through the MDF to get the blade into the gaps in the middle of the hanger.)

BRIGHT IDEAS

If you don't want to risk slowly unpicking all your clothes each time you use these hangers, it would probably be a good idea to sand the edges.

MATERIALS & EQUIPMENT

Coat-hanger (for template)
Pencil
1cm (¼in) MDF or ply (you'll get eight
   hangers from one 2.4x1.2m (8x4ft) sheet)

Photocopied face
Scissors or craft knife
Jigsaw with timber-cutting blade
Drill with 10mm wood bit
Rubber glue or PVA

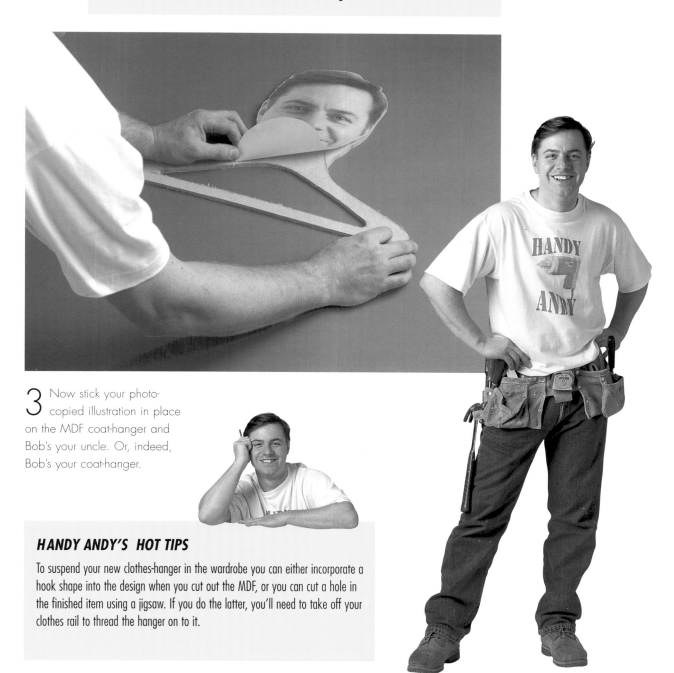

3 Now stick your photo-
copied illustration in place
on the MDF coat-hanger and
Bob's your uncle. Or, indeed,
Bob's your coat-hanger.

HANDY ANDY'S HOT TIPS

To suspend your new clothes-hanger in the wardrobe you can either incorporate a
hook shape into the design when you cut out the MDF, or you can cut a hole in
the finished item using a jigsaw. If you do the latter, you'll need to take off your
clothes rail to thread the hanger on to it.

false-depth alcove shelves

Here's a trick for giving boring old shelves a bit more 'weight'. A false panel added to the front of each span will make these shelves look deeper and more expensive than they really are. Better still, the front panel makes the shelves strong enough to cope with a whole alphabet of encyclopedias. This clever project will turn your alcove into a very stylish storage area.

1 Use a spirit level to help measure and mark out positions for the battens that will support each shelf. Cut your battens 2.5cm (1in) less than the depth of the finished shelves, or angle the ends so they won't interfere with the facing strips when they're in place. Then *Plug/Screw* them on to the walls on either side of the alcove.

MATERIALS & EQUIPMENT

Tape measure
Pencil
Spirit level
60cm (2ft) of 5x2.5cm (2x1in) timber batten per shelf
Handsaw or jigsaw with timber-cutting blade
Drill with 6mm masonry bit and

3mm wood bit for pilot holes
Bradawl
6mm wall plugs (solid or cavity)
Screwdriver or screwdriver bit for drill
4.5cm (1¾in) size 8 wood screws
2cm (¾in) MDF or ply (about one 2.4mx1.2m (8x4ft) sheet)
Sliding bevel
Wood glue

2 Measure and cut your shelves from the MDF. Remember that the alcove may not be square and may not even be the same shape or size all the way up, so use some care (or better still, a sliding bevel) to make sure each shelf is cut to fit its chosen position. A sliding bevel can be locked off at any angle and that setting used to transfer the measurement to the material you are cutting to fit.

3 Cut 7.5cm (3in) strips of MDF the same width as each shelf, then *Glue/Screw* them in place along the underside of the front edge.

The false-depth trick is not just for homebuilt shelves of course — it works just as well on new flatpack units or existing bookcases. Take a look around the house and see if you have any boring old shallow shelves that would benefit from a bit of added depth in their lives.

4 Once complete, simply rest your finished shelves in place on top of the battens. If you didn't use a spirit level to ensure that your measurements where perfectly horizontal, both left to right and front to back, this is when you'll wish you had. Assuming they are straight, there's no need to secure the shelves in place, and leaving them loose means that you can easily take them off for painting.

shaker-style peg rail

In the bedroom, in the bathroom, behind the front door or even next to the cooker – everyone needs a peg rail now and then, and what better design than the classic simplicity of your very own Shaker style? Made to measure and built to last these rails can be designed to cope with anything from a cramped cupboard to an entire wall. This project is almost as easy to make as it is to use and will give you something both practical and attractive to look at, when it's not laden with junk that is...

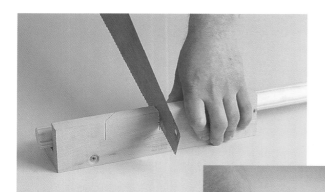

1 Measure and cut the planed batten timber to the size of rail you require, then drill 2.5cm (1in) holes all the way through it using a spade bit at intervals of 10–15cm (4–6in). (A 'spade bit' is a large drill that is flat rather than round.) The holes should all be drilled either square on or at the same slight angle so that things don't fall off your finished pegs!

2 Cut your pegs from the timber dowelling. It's best to use the 90° slot in a mitre cutting block to ensure your pegs come out nice and straight. Our pegs were about 15cm (6in) long, but they can be however long you want: just make sure they're all the same!

MATERIALS & EQUIPMENT

Tape measure
Pencil
About 120cm (4ft) of 5x5cm (2x2in) planed timber batten
Handsaw or jigsaw with timber-cutting blade
Drill with 6mm masonry bit, 3mm wood bit and 2.5cm (1in) spade bit for peg holes
2.5cm (1in) dowelling (allow about 20cm (8in) per peg)
Mitre block
Sandpaper
Wood glue
Hammer
Spirit level with timber straight edge
Bradawl
Paint or varnish
6mm wall plugs (solid or cavity)
4.5cm (1¾in) size 8 wood screws or dome-head screws
Wood filler (optional)

4 Use a dab of glue and a hammer to secure the pegs into the rail. Don't hammer hard on the bare peg if it won't go in easily; put a block of scrap wood between the hammer and peg to protect the peg's end from damage. Drill about four thin screw holes through the peg rail, then use these holes to mark drilling points on the wall behind. Use a spirit level to make sure the rail goes on straight. Paint or varnish all the wood, then *Plug/Screw* the finished peg rail in place. Fill the screwhead holes and smooth over before painting. Alternatively, use some dome-head screws if they're going to remain on show.

3 Use some sandpaper to smooth off the sawn edges at both ends of each peg.

magic shelves

Look, no hands! And no brackets either. These great-looking and apparently unsupported shelves are ideal for lights, ornaments and decoration, but don't be tempted to load them up with that set of encyclopedias you've just bought. Striking they may be, sturdy they are not. For safety's sake you're best limiting the length of these shelves to about 30cm (12in) if you don't want to place too much strain on the batten and too much broken crockery on the floor.

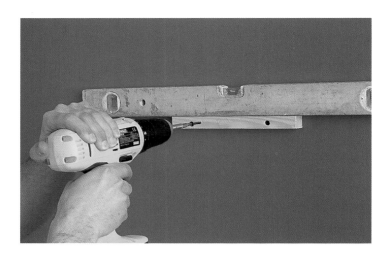

MATERIALS & EQUIPMENT

Tape measure
Pencil
2.5x2.5cm (1x1in) timber batten (long
   enough for each shelf)
Handsaw or jigsaw with timber-cutting blade
Drill with 6mm masonry bit and 3mm wood bit
   for pilot holes
Spirit level
Bradawl
6mm wall plugs (solid or cavity)
Screwdriver or screwdriver bit for drill
4.5cm (1¾in) size 10 wood screws (for the
   battens)
20x7.5cm (8x3in) new or scrap timber (allow
   30cm (12in) maximum per shelf)
Router with rebate-cutter bit
Wood glue
7.5cm (3in) size 8 wood screws (for the shelves)

1 Measure and cut timber battens the same length as your intended shelves. Drill two screw holes through each batten and position them on the wall, using a spirit level to get them straight. Use the screw holes to mark drilling points on the wall, then *Plug/Screw* the battens in place.

BRIGHT IDEAS

Sand off any rough edges if you want a smoother finish to your timber. You might like to experiment with some wood varnish or paint to create your own look.

This sort of shelf looks very nice on its own, but a little group of them arranged on the wall looks even better.

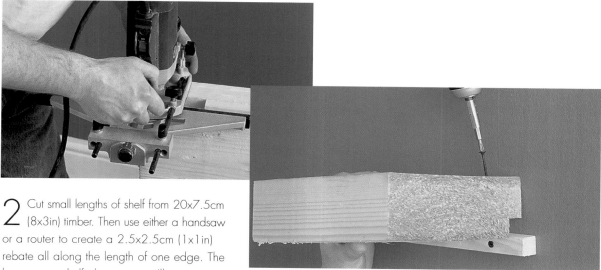

2 Cut small lengths of shelf from 20x7.5cm (8x3in) timber. Then use either a handsaw or a router to create a 2.5x2.5cm (1x1in) rebate all along the length of one edge. The longer your shelf, the more you'll appreciate a router to do this task. Once the material is held firmly in place and the sliding guide on the router is set to 2.5cm (1in), it's simply a matter of running the tool along the timber to create a perfect rebate.

3 Glue the shelves on to each batten so that the batten fits snugly into the rebate, then screw down through the top rear edge using 7.5cm (3in) screws. Make sure these screws end up flush with the surface.

ornate mirror frame

Most people tend to buy mirrors with the frame already attached, but if you can get mirror glass direct from a glass merchant, or you have an old mirror with a damaged frame, this is the project for you. The motif *Changing Rooms* designer Linda Barker created here is great, but there's nothing to stop you creating whatever shape you want and adapting it to suit any room.

MATERIALS & EQUIPMENT

1.25cm (½in) MDF or ply (at least 15cm (6in) bigger than your mirror all round)
Pencil
Paper for template
Tape measure
Jigsaw with scroll-cutting blade

Drill with 10mm wood bit for jigsaw pilot hole
Sandpaper
Screwdriver
4 mirror clips and accompanying screws
2 screw eyelets
Wire or strong string for hanging

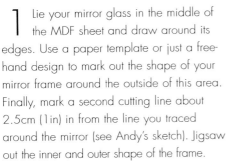

1 Lie your mirror glass in the middle of the MDF sheet and draw around its edges. Use a paper template or just a free-hand design to mark out the shape of your mirror frame around the outside of this area. Finally, mark a second cutting line about 2.5cm (1in) in from the line you traced around the mirror (see Andy's sketch). Jigsaw out the inner and outer shape of the frame.

2 Sand all the edges smooth: boring, but necessary, I'm afraid. If you want to paint your frame, do it now before the mirror glass gets in the way.

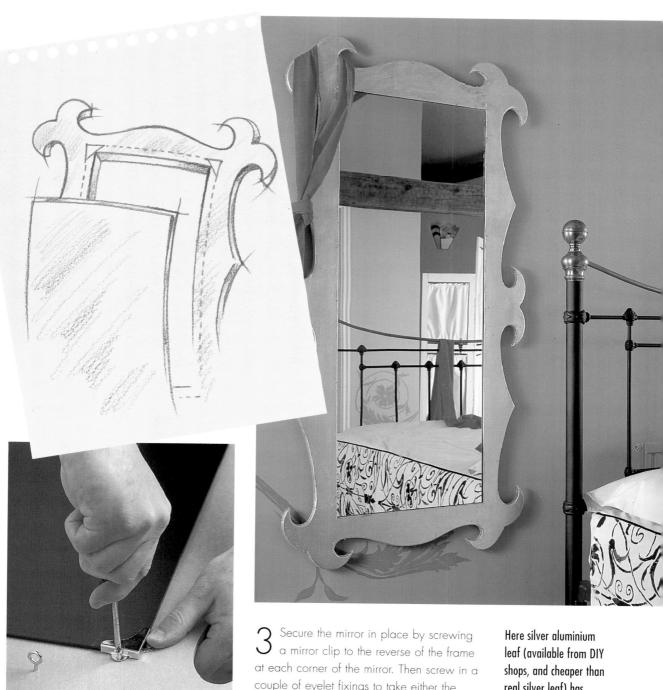

3 Secure the mirror in place by screwing a mirror clip to the reverse of the frame at each corner of the mirror. Then screw in a couple of eyelet fixings to take either the string or wire that will support the mirror when it's up. Check that all your fixings are secure, then hang the mirror on the wall using a plugged screw or specialist fixing. If you can see yourself, it's the right way round.

Here silver aluminium leaf (available from DIY shops, and cheaper than real silver leaf) has been applied to the frame. A coat of clear varnish was applied over it for protection.

revamped wardrobe doors

Okay – let's say you've already got a wardrobe. Let's say you really hate it, but can't afford another one just yet. No problem. Some new chicken wire, some old fabric, a bit of scrap architrave, and you're laughing. Just add green wellies and spread out some silage to complete the country feeling.

MATERIALS & EQUIPMENT

Screwdriver or screwdriver bit for drill

Tape measure

Pencil

Drill with 10mm wood bit for jigaw pilot hole

Jigsaw with timber-cutting blade

Sandpaper

Pliers or tin snips

Chicken wire (enough to cover each door)

Staple gun and staples or 'U'-shaped staples to be hammered in

2.5cm (1in) panel pins

Hammer

Fabric (enough to cover each door)

Fabric glue (optional)

5cm (2in) architrave (to go around the top and possibly the bottom of the wardrobe)

Mitre block

Wood glue

Nail punch

This wardrobe was finished with a distressed paint effect (see page 33) for a 'country' feel.

1 Take the doors off your wardrobe using a screwdriver and carefully mark out a line about 5cm (2in) in from the edge of the existing mouldings. Use a jigsaw to cut out the resulting shape in each panel. To start the cut, drill a pilot hole in the unwanted part of each panel to insert the saw blade. Alternatively, if your wardrobe doors are truly hideous, buy replacement doors from a DIY supplier.

2 Sand the inner edges of these new holes to make them smooth, and touch up any of the paintwork you might have damaged along the way.

3 Using a pair of pliers or tin snips, cut out pieces of chicken wire about 2.5cm (1in) wider all round than the holes in the door panels. Working on the inside of the door, pin or staple a piece of chicken wire to the back of each hole (ensuring the wire is taut across the hole). Next, pin, staple or even glue your chosen pieces of fabric to hang behind the wire. The fabric can be flat or gathered. Put the revamped doors back on the wardrobe.

SAFETY TIP

Chicken wire is not for the faint-hearted: the ends are sharp and will catch on virtually anything they touch. To make sure all your clothes come out of the wardrobe in one piece, bend the edges of the chicken wire under before you fasten it down. Also, for a more durable and attractive result, cut your fabric slightly larger than you need and hem the edges before you secure it in place.

4 Mitre the ends of three lengths of archi-trave (which correspond in length to the front and sides of your wardrobe). Fix the architrave to the top of the wardrobe with wood glue, then hammer in several panel pins to secure it firmly in place. Use a nail punch to make sure your panel pins disap-pear into the architrave. If there's room beneath the wardrobe doors, you can fix some more architrave along the bottom too.

footwell floor surround

One of you wants carpet in the bedroom, the other wants a hard floor. Guess what? It's your lucky day. This somewhat unusual project can bring a familiar old room to life or salvage a carpet that is either too small for the room you have in mind or damaged around the edge. The size of the border can be adjusted to fit whatever carpet you have.

MATERIALS & EQUIPMENT

Tape measure
Pencil
10cm (4in) or 15cm (6in) tongue-
    and-groove planks (enough to fit
    around your room as a 90cm (3ft)
    wide border)
Handsaw or jigsaw with timber-
    cutting blade
Mitre block

Sliding bevel
Wood glue
4cm (1½in) lost head nails
Hammer
Nail punch
Acrylic varnish
Paintbrush
Carpet knife
Double-sided carpet tape or nailed
    carpet-gripper strips

1 Clear the room, carpet and all, so that you can mark out a line about 90cm (3ft) in from the walls all the way around. Always keep your lines parallel to the walls, even if the corners aren't exactly 90° angles. Measure the lengths of your walls from corner to corner and cut the floorboards to be positioned nearest to the walls accordingly. Mitre cut the ends of each board where they meet at the corners using a mitre block (see page 15). Remember, don't just assume that every corner is a right angle. Check it out with a sliding bevel before you cut. To ensure your mitre cuts line up even if the room is not square, cut each board only after you have cut and nailed the previous one in place. That way you'll know exactly what angle you have to match.

2 Working from the wall inwards, glue and then nail the first line of floorboards into place against the walls. Use plenty of glue in all the grooves and along the ends of each plank.

You don't have to use tongue-and-groove boards. If you don't mind seeing the fixing head marks when you're, finished you could nail or screw down conventional planks instead.

3 To cleverly disguise your fixing technique, nail the boards down through the tongues about every 15cm (6in); the nails will be hidden by the groove of the adjacent board. Make sure you drive the nails in at an angle that will not obstruct the next board slotting into place and everything will be neatly hidden away as you progress. If you haven't got a hammer shaped to get the nail heads right into the wood, you can always drive them that last little bit by holding another blunt nail on top and hammering this a couple of times. Alternatively, use a proper nail punch.

4 Once the wooden surround is in place, apply a coat of acrylic varnish to seal and protect it. Allow at least two hours' drying time. Measure the gap in the middle of the room and cut the carpet to fit. Use either double-sided carpet tape or nailed gripper strips to hold the carpet in place.

colour-washed floorboards

Underneath the most tasteless and disgusting carpet could lie the possibility of a fantastic floor finish. Have a peek. If you've got floorboards rather than concrete down there, it's off with the carpet, on with the face mask and hello dust storm. Once sanded, you can either seal the boards with varnish straight away, or do as we did and add a colour-wash effect first. Don't worry if your floor is patchy, the sander will cut through dirt and old varnish to bring all the timber up to more or less the same colour.

1 Clear the room and carefully check the whole floor for loose boards or projecting nail heads and staples. Remove or hammer down all protrusions (with a hammer and nail punch) and screw down any loose boards to provide a perfectly smooth and solid surface.

2 Use a hired floor sander and edger combination to smooth off the floorboards. You should start with the large floor sander, working across the grain first with coarse and then medium sandpapers. Always finish off along the grain with a fine paper.

3 Go all around the edge of the f using the same technique as ab with the little sander.

MATERIALS & EQUIPMENT

Claw hammer
Nail punch (optional)
Screwdriver
Wood screws
Upright and hand-held floor sanders
Coarse, medium and fine sandpaper
Emulsion paint
Paintbrushes
Acrylic varnish

4 Mix together your favourite colour emulsion paint with the same amount of water, then brush quickly on to the floorboards along the grain. The more water you use in this mixture, the more subtle the final colour. Once dry (an hour after painting), give the floor a couple of coats of varnish.

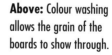

Above: Colour washing allows the grain of the boards to show through.

Above: For a bleached-effect floor, sand and then brush dilute white acrylic primer over the boards.

Right: To produce mock-grained floorboards, rock a woodgraining rocker over wet glazed boards.

RECEPTION ROOMS

Once you are confident enough with your DIY skills to 'go public' there's a wealth of floorspace out there just waiting for your tool toting talents. The living room, the dining room, even the hall or the landing, they've all got walls and windows, and sad little spaces that crave your affection.

fretwork radiator cover

There was a time when pre-cut fretwork panels were available only to those in the know. Nowadays, more and more of the big DIY stores are stocking a whole variety of them and opening up endless home building possibilities for all of us. This project uses a lovely piece of decorative screening called Jali fretwork to hide a shabby old radiator.

1 Measure your radiator and add 15cm (6in) all round (to leave room for the valves at each side and enough space for heat to circulate above). Mark these measurements on the MDF and cut out the rectangle with a jigsaw. You need to cut both an inner and outer frame from this piece of MDF to create the front of the radiator cover. To do this mark out a rectangle 5cm (2in) from the top and sides of this panel, but 12.5cm (5in) in from the bottom. Then draw a second rectangle 5cm (2in) inside this. Now carefully cut out the inner frame, first making a thin drill hole in which to start off the blade. You are going to need both the inner frame and the outer frame later on, so make sure you don't bodge the cutting.

MATERIALS & EQUIPMENT

Tape measure
Pencil
2cm (¾in) MDF or ply (about one
  2.4x1.2m (8x4ft) sheet)
Handsaw or jigsaw with timber-
  cutting blade
Drill with 3mm wood bit for starting
  jigsaw cut
Wood glue
Screwdriver or screwdriver bit
3cm (1¼in) size 8 wood screws
for MDF assembly

Fretwork panel (large enough to
  cover the radiator)
1cm (½in) size 6 wood screws for
  fretwork panel assembly
15cm (6in) Torus skirting board
  (enough to go around the radiator
  cover)
5cm (2in) Ogee architrave (enough
  to go around the radiator cover)
Panel pins
Pin hammer
Nail punch
2 magnetic catches

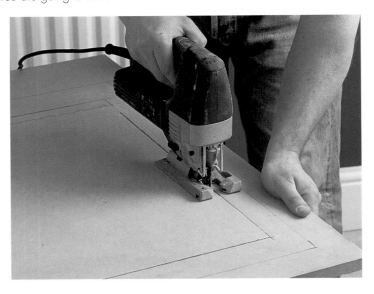

Decorative fretwork panels are available in several patterns, all begging to be used in some creative DIY project. Racked alongside them you might also see some punched metal panels which are just crying out to be incorporated into a high-tech variation of this project.

2 Measure the distance your radiator projects from the wall, then add 5cm (2in) to this measurement. Mark out the top and side panels of your cover to this width on the MDF, then cut out with a jigsaw. *Glue/Screw* these panels on to the back of your outer frame to form the carcass of the cover. Cut four small triangles of MDF to form the backstops for your fretwork panel and *Glue/Screw* them behind each corner of the frame.

HANDY ANDY'S HOT TIPS

You don't have to make your cover exactly 15cm (6in) larger than your radiator all round if that creates space problems. However, you must leave at least 5cm (2in) all round to let the heat circulate and escape into your room.

3 Cut your fretwork panel so that it is 2.5cm (1in) smaller than the inner frame all the way round, then *Glue/Screw* it on to the back of that inner frame. Make sure it's straight before you put in the second screw! Don't forget to drill pilot holes for each screw to stop the fretwork splitting as you work.

4 To complete the carcass, measure a length of skirting board to fit around the three sides of the cover flush with the bottom edge. You can create your mitre cuts quickly if you have a jigsaw or circular saw that can be locked in a 45° cutting position. Otherwise you'll have to mark up the skirting with a pencil and resort to a handsaw. Once cut, *Glue/Screw* the skirting into place from the back so that you don't have to fill the holes later on. Don't worry that the skirting is slightly higher than the bottom of the outer frame – it's meant to be like that. In combination with the little triangles you fitted earlier, this will form the slot in which the fretwork panel will sit.

5 Repeat the whole process by securing some 5cm (2in) architrave around the top of the radiator cover to complete the effect. This can simply be glued and pinned into place if you've had enough screwing for one day.

BRIGHT IDEAS

If you have a large radiator to hide, you can improve the design of your cover by creating two or three panels spaced evenly across the front.

6 The fretwork panel should now sit in place between the protruding skirting at the front and the MDF wedges at the back. This panel can be easily removed so that you can still get to the valves at either end of the radiator: simply screw a couple of magnetic door catches into the MDF to hold the fretwork panel in place. The cover itself is not fixed to the wall – it just sits on the floor.

tiled fire surround

Tiling. Arghhh! Everyone thinks laying tiles is an absolute nightmare, but in truth it's just like every other DIY project. So long as you have the right tools, the right materials and the right technique, it's a doddle – honest. Here's a small fire surround project just to get you started. Quite apart from the fact that this project looks great when it's finished, tiling also provides one of the most hard-working and easy-to-clean surfaces around. Perfect for any fireplace fall-out.

MATERIALS & EQUIPMENT

Tape measure
Pencil
Spirit level with timber straight edge
Ready-mixed or powdered tile adhesive
 (with spreader)
12.5x12.5cm (5x5in) tiles (according to your
 fire surround area)
Tile-spacers (4 per tile)
Tile-cutter or tile-scorer
Ready-mixed or powdered tile grout
Damp cloth

1 Prepare the area to be tiled so that it is flat and smooth. Use a pencil and a spirit level to mark everything out before you start; that way you'll notice if things go out of line long before you've put any tiles in place. If you can dictate how big an area you intend to cover (just part of a wall rather than the whole thing), make sure that the dimensions suit the size of your tiles. If you can't dictate the area, always start tiling from the middle and work outwards.

Once you've got the bug and the technique for tiling, why not look a little further afield to exploit your new-found talents. Perhaps you could extend your design down on to the hearth area, or even up on to the mantelpiece? There are endless tile designs to play with if you want to mix and match your colours and patterns a bit.

2 Okay, here we go. Don't rush. Using a proper serrated spreader, spread out enough adhesive for 4 or 5 tiles at a time. Press your tiles carefully into place and as you stick each one down, insert a little plastic spacer at each corner of the tile to keep all the gaps even. Don't assume you can manage without tile-spacers – you can't.

3 When you come to a tile that needs cutting, always measure it carefully first. To make the cuts it's best to use a proper tile-cutting tool. This has a sharp metal wheel which you simply draw across your tile in one firm movement. You then snap the tile along that line. The tile-cutter is mounted on a rigid frame, which makes it easy to line your tiles up straight for each cut. If you're confident enough, you can do without a tile-cutter and simply scratch a line across your tile with a tile-scoring tool. You then snap it over a matchstick.

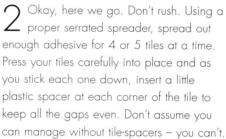

BRIGHT IDEAS

If your tiles aren't fitted flush to the wall, you can always finish off your new fire surround with some 5cm (2in) architrave around the outside edges. Measure the sides and top of the tiled area. Cut the architrave to the required length using a mitre to obtain 45° angles for the top left and right corners. Glue and panel pin the architrave in place.

4 Once the adhesive has dried for about an hour (check the manufacturer's recommendations on the packaging for drying times), spread a load of grout over the tiles and quickly use a damp cloth to wipe off anything that hasn't gone down into the gaps. Let the whole thing go off (set) overnight before you treat it with any dis-respect. That's it. You're a tiler.

personalized pelmet

For the most part, a nice pair of curtains really look the business, but sometimes it would be nice to lose all that bunched-up stuff at the top. Here's the answer – a pelmet, but not just any old pelmet. Here's one that you can actually add your own design to. Whether you are after simple curves or elaborate scrolls, this project will put you a jigsaw blade away from the window furniture of your dreams.

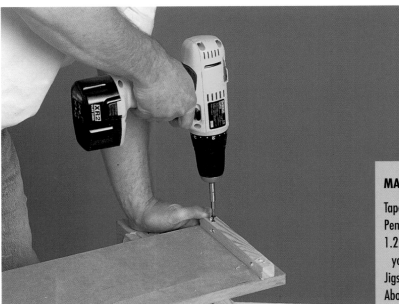

The decoration is fairly conservative here, but you could use a deeper panel and experiment with more dramatic cuts. How about V-shaped spikes, or even a hint of spiral at each end?

MATERIALS & EQUIPMENT

Tape measure
Pencil
1.25cm (½in) MDF or ply (long enough to span your window and create the sides of the pelmet)
Jigsaw with timber-cutting blade
About 90cm (3ft) of 2.5x2.5cm (1x1in) timber batten
Wood glue
Drill with 6mm masonry bit
Bradawl or 3mm wood bit for pilot holes
Screwdriver or screwdriver bit for drill
3cm (1¼in) size 8 wood screws for MDF assembly
Paper for template
Sandpaper
Spirit level with timber straight edge
6mm wall plugs (solid or cavity)
4cm (1½in) size 8 wood screws for attaching battens to wall

1 Measure the width of your window opening and add 15cm (6in) at each end – this is the length of the front panel. The depth of the panel is up to you, but as a guide, we made our pelmet 20cm (8in) deep. Cut out the front and side panels from the MDF. The width of the side panels can vary – ours were 20cm (8in) deep and 15cm (6in) wide. Cut out two battens to match the depth of your curtain pelmet and *Glue/Screw* these along each end of the front panel.

BRIGHT IDEAS

We have limited our pelmet design to the front panel only, but it would look great if the shapes you create start on the front, but then continue around to include the two side panels as well. You might even want to make your side panels longer, so that they drop significantly further down the wall than the rest of the pelmet. This would allow you to create a very dramatic shape indeed.

2 *Glue/Screw* the side panels to the battens attached to the front panel. Always put your screws through from the back, that way you won't leave any ugly screwhead marks that will need to be filled before you paint.

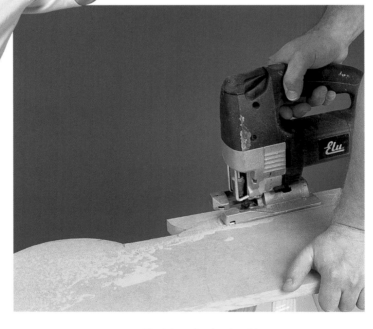

3 Now the fun bit. Using a paper template or freehand design, draw a decorative edge along the bottom of the front panel. Cut along this line with a jigsaw and sand off any rough edges.

HANDY ANDY'S HOT TIPS

Once the construction phase is over, your pelmet can be completed in one of two ways. First, you can create a flat colour or paint-effect finish to complement the surrounding walls. Or, second, you can cover the whole thing in fabric that is designed to match or contrast with the curtains below. Whichever option you go with, the whole process is far easier and quicker when tackled on the ground rather than at the top of a step-ladder.

4 Use your finished pelmet as a guide to mark out positions for two timber wall battens, which will fit inside the pelmet side panels. Position them so that the centres of the battens align with the top of the window. Check with a spirit level that they're straight, then *Plug/Screw* them to the wall. Always drill pilot holes through your battens before driving in the actual screws: it makes everything far easier and far more accurate.

5 Hold the pelmet up to the wall so that the battens fit inside and align with the side panels. *Glue/Screw* the battens to the pelmet side panels from inside the pelmet.

tongue-and-groove table-top

This is a great project for hiding a scruffy old table or increasing the size of one which you've now outgrown. However, always make sure the legs of your existing table are of a sound and solid construction before you ask them to carry the additional weight and responsibility of a major family gathering.

MATERIALS & EQUIPMENT

Tape measure
Pencil
10cm (4in) or 15cm (6in) tongue-and-groove
   floorboards (enough to cover your old table-
   top with a 10cm (4in) overlap all round)
Handsaw or jigsaw with timber-cutting blade
Wood glue
2 sash clamps
5x2.5cm (2x1in) timber batten (enough to
   run twice the length and twice the width of
   your old table-top)
4cm (1½in) size 8 wood screws
Drill with 3mm wood bit for pilot holes
Screwdriver or screwdriver bit for drill

1 Measure your old table-top, then add 10cm (4in) extra on all sides. Cut enough tongue-and-groove planks of equal length to cover the total area of the table. Use a proper wood adhesive to glue the planks side by side, and try to get hold of some sash clamps to hold everything rigid while it dries.

2 Once dry, place your new tabletop face down and lie the old table on top of it, right in the middle. Mark around the edge of your old table-top, then remove it.

The real beauty of this project is that nothing is fixed into place for good. If you need a larger table only when all the family come round for lunch, but want the space back when they've gone, this is the perfect solution. Just slide the new table-top under a bed when it's not required for entertaining.

3 Cut out four timber battens to fit the lines you have just drawn, then *Glue/Screw* them to the underside of your new table-top. Make sure you don't use screws which are longer than the depth of the batten and plank combined! This border will not only help hold the tongue-and-groove planks together, but will fit snugly over the existing table-top to stop any movement.

4 Turn everything the right way up and lower your new top into place. If you don't want to paint or varnish the wood, you should at least protect it from food and drink stains by applying a coat of Danish Oil.

classical mantel-shelf

Mantelpieces make a nice display area for lamps and ornaments, and are a useful surface to leave your cups of tea on! With this project you can not only build one from scratch in about half an hour, but you can also make it look as though it's been there since the Romans were last in town. The decorative supports, known as 'corbels', are available from most decent hardware shops and come in a load of different shapes and sizes. They are usually made of plaster, but some specialist suppliers still make them out of wood if you want that particular look.

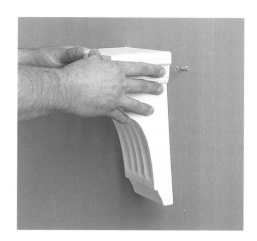

HANDY ANDY'S HOT TIPS

Ideally, the corbels should be placed so that they're the same distance apart as the size of your fireplace opening, but their optimum position depends on how big you want the finished mantelshelf to be. For maximum strength the shelf needs to be supported at two points about a quarter of the full length in from each end, but you can play with this guide a fair bit to ensure the final effect looks right in relation to your fireplace. If you need a span wider than about 120cm (4ft) between the corbels, or want the shelf to hold some particularly heavy ornaments, upgrade your timber or MDF to something a bit thicker. Heightwise, I reckon that if you place the corbels so that their bottom edge is level with the top of your fireplace opening, the appearance will look bang on.

Obviously, nobody's going to come round and sue you if you decide to use this idea somewhere other than your fireplace. It will make a very elegant shelving solution in any of your rooms, and if you want a really dramatic effect, simply construct two or three shelves above each other to double or triple the impact.

1 On the back of each corbel is a small mounting plate designed to slip over the head of a nail or screw. Measure where these mounting plates are in relation to the top and bottom of your corbels and then using a spirit level and a rule calculate where your fixing screws will have to be on the wall to support your corbels at the exact height you want them. Drill and plug your holes then drive in some 2cm (¾in) size 10 screws, leaving the heads far enough out to catch on the mounting plates. Add some panel adhesive to the back of each corbel.

MATERIALS & EQUIPMENT

Rule
Pencil
Spirit level with timber straight edge
2 plaster or wooden corbels
Drill with 6mm masonry bit
Screwdriver or screwdriver bit for drill
6mm wall plugs (solid or cavity, for corbels)
2cm (¾in) size 10 wood screws (for corbels)
Panel adhesive
15x2.5cm (6x1in) timber for shelf
   (or 15x2cm (6x¾in) MDF)
Handsaw or jigsaw with timber-cutting blade
3mm wood bit for pilot holes
4cm (1½in) size 8 wood screws (optional)

2 For the shelf itself, measure and cut timber or MDF to length. The front of the shelf should project about 5cm (2in) beyond the corbels. Use panel adhesive to secure the finished shelf to each corbel, or screws if your corbels are wooden.

scrap timber shelves

There are two things that just about every DIY project will generate: bad language and scrap timber. Your family will have to deal with the first, but here's a neat little project to deal with the second. You always need the odd shelf around the house, and here's one which is as odd as they come. It's entirely made from leftovers, sculptured brackets and all.

These brackets can be made much bigger than shown here. Just imagine the effect of long, tapering ones. Remember to maintain a sense of scale, and keep the length and thickness of the shelf in balance with the longer brackets.

MATERIALS & EQUIPMENT

Tape measure
Pencil
Chunky scrap timber (to make brackets, and
    shelves about 90cm (3ft) long)
Jigsaw with timber-cutting blade
Wood glue
Drill with 3mm wood bit for
    pilot holes
7.5cm (3in) size 8 wood screws
Screwdriver or screwdriver bit for drill
Clamps
Spirit level with timber straight edge
Bradawl
6mm masonry bit for drill
6mm wood plugs (solid or cavity)
Wood filler
Sandpaper

1 Take some chunky bits of scrap timber and mark out the shape of the supporting brackets you want. Cut out pairs of identical pieces. For 90cm (3ft) shelves, make the brackets about 15cm (6in) high and 10cm (4in) deep. To make all the brackets the same shape use a paper template to mark up your timber before each cut.

A simple lick of acrylic varnish or some water-based stain will protect your shelves without losing the original grain of the timber. If, however, your wood is too far gone to remain on show in its 'birthday suit' finish, plug the big holes and knocks with filler and then disguise everything with a couple of layers of paint.

HANDY ANDY'S HOT TIPS

If the scrap timber you have is too thin, stick several bits together before you start cutting out. You could, of course, use new timber of the right size, but that kind of defeats the object of this exercise, doesn't it?

2 *Glue/Screw* the pairs together and clamp them tight while the adhesive dries.

3 Drill two holes right through each bracket from the front: one should be 2.5cm (1in) from the bottom and the other 5cm (2in) from the bottom. Then use a spirit level to mark fixing positions on the wall. *Plug/Screw* the brackets in place through the drilled holes. Make sure your screwheads lie flush with the timber when you're done.

4 Use more scrap timber to make a shelf. This should be cut so that it projects beyond the brackets by about 2.5cm (1in) at the front and 7.5cm (3in) at each end. Drill a pilot hole through the shelf over each bracket and screw it into place. Fill all your screw holes with wood filler, sand everything down and finish off with a lick of paint.

alcove display unit

If you have a fireplace, chances are you've got an alcove or two. The easy but messy way of using them is to stack them high with junk. The conventional but boring thing to do is fill them with shelves. The inspired alternative is to have a go at building this very unusual alcove unit that *Changing Rooms* designer Graham Wynne dreamt up. Trust me, it's not as complicated as it looks.

MATERIALS & EQUIPMENT

Tape measure
Pencil
2cm (¾in) MDF or ply (about two 2.4x1.2m
   (8x4ft) sheets)
Drill with10mm wood bit for jigsaw pilot hole
Jigsaw with timber-cutting blade
5x2.5cm (2x1in) timber batten (enough to
   go all around the alcove)
3mm wood bit for pilot holes
6mm masonry bit
6mm wall plugs (solid or cavity)
4cm (1½in) size 8 wood screws
Screwdriver or screwdriver bit for drill
2.5x2.5cm (1x1in) timber batten (enough to
   go all around each hole)
Wood glue

1 Measure the width and height of your alcove and cut your sheet of MDF exactly to these measurements. Mark out a square on the MDF panel. We marked up a square 30x30cm (12x12in) right in the centre of the panel, but there's nothing to stop you cutting out two or three squares to make several shelves if the fancy takes you (see overleaf).

This alcove idea isn't limited to being used on either side of a chimney breast — it can be applied to any nook or cranny. Just so long as you have secure fixing points on the floor, the ceiling and one side of any opening, the world is your oyster...

HANDY ANDY'S HOT TIPS

Not for the faint-hearted this one...
You can create a dramatic variation
on this project by sloping the entire
alcove unit so that it appears to be
leaning back against the wall.
You'll need to measure and mount
your main panel so that the
bottom is out level with the front
of the alcove and the top is
against the back wall. Mounting
the wall battens at an angle
down each side is pretty
straightforward, but recalcu-
lating the shape of your
boxes so that they still
remain level all the way up
amounts to rocket science
if you ask me.

You can display even
more of your favourite
objects with these two
neat ideas for a three-
shelf alcove project.

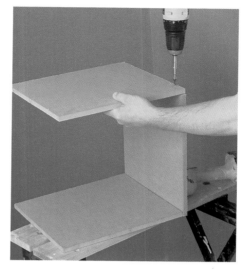

2 Cut two 5x2.5cm (2x1in) timber battens to match
the depth of the alcove, and two battens to match
the width. *Plug/Screw* the long battens to each side of
the alcove and the short battens to the bottom and top of
it. (You won't need to use plugs in the floor if it's made of
wood.) The battens should be fixed at the same distance
from the back of the alcove
unless you want a
skewed unit.

3 Measure the depth from the front of
these battens to the back of your alcove
and use this figure to make up a square
MDF box with no top or bottom.
Glue/Screw the box together with no
battens for now: the
box will become
rigid once it is fixed
to the front panel.

BRIGHT IDEAS

If you are feeling particularly adventurous, you can have some
lighting wired in behind this unit. (Remember always to consult a
qualified electrician when installing lighting.) The shelf boxes will
need to be made a good few inches shallower than the depth of
the alcove and you will need to give them some kind of translu-
cent backing, such as tracing paper, to allow the light through.
You will also need to make this backing removable so that you
can reach through to change the bulbs occasionally; try using
velcro tape for easy access.

4 Once the box
is complete,
cut lengths of
2.5x2.5cm (1x1in)
timber batten to
match the sides of
the hole in the alcove. Using these battens,
Glue/Screw the box to the front panel
around the hole and let all the adhesive dry
thoroughly. Your alcove unit is now ready to
screw into place. Make some pilot holes
through the main panel before you
Glue/Screw it to the battens on the walls,
ceiling and floor.

block shelving

There are loads of brilliant materials in the building trade, but most of them spend their lives lost inside the structure of your house and never see the light of day. Well, here are two we've set free to start the revolution. Take one brick starter grid and some concrete blocks, add a little MDF and hey presto – you have a shelving unit straight out of New York's trendiest loft apartment.

1 Place two brick starter grids on the wall about 90cm (3ft) apart, use a spirit level to check that they're aligned, then secure them in place with the fixings provided. Loose stack either concrete or thermolite blocks to calculate how high you want the unit and how many shelves you're going to build in. We stacked the blocks two deep between shelves, and took them right up to the ceiling. Once you're happy with your arrangement, mix up a bucket of mortar and start laying the blocks in place for real.

2 The brick starter grid has tabs that fold down across each block, tying the whole construction firmly to the wall. Use a pair of pliers to prise these down over the blocks. Measure the distance between the outside edges of each stack of bricks and add on 10cm (4in) each end – this will be the length of your shelves. Measure from the front edge of the blocks to the wall and add on 1.25cm (½in) for the width of the shelves. Cut out as many shelves as you need from MDF using these measurements.

MATERIALS & EQUIPMENT

Tape measure
Pencil
2 brick starter grids (with fixing
  nails)
Spirit level with timber straight
  edge
Hammer
Concrete or thermolite blocks
Mortar mix
Trowel
Pliers
1.25cm (½in) MDF or ply
  (about two 2.4x1.2m
(8x4ft) sheets)
Handsaw or jigsaw with
  timber-cutting blade
2.5cm (1in) panel pins
Wood glue

BRIGHT IDEAS

If your shelves are going to carry a lot of weight, use 2cm (¾in) MDF for the construction for greater strength.

Personally, I love the high-tech/industrial style of these shelves, but it's not going to be suited to every home. If you really fancy trying this project but don't have the interior to match, think about using it for tool storage in the garage or even for a new set of shelves in the cellar. Why not go mad and try it in the bathroom?

3 When the blocks are two deep on either side, put a final layer of mortar on each brick. Hammer the panel pins part way through the MDF shelves where you want to attach them to the bricks before you lay the shelves on to the wet mortar. Then finish hammering the pins through the MDF into the mortar. As you place each shelf on the mortar, check with a spirit level that it's straight before you move on.

4 Finally, cut strips of the narrow MDF 5cm (2in) wide and the length and depth of your shelves, then glue and pin them along the front and sides of each shelf. This makes the whole thing look a lot more professional, but leave the mortar to dry overnight before you fix these strips in place.

fretwork TV cabinet

I love looking at the TV when it's on, but I'm not so keen on staring at it when it's switched off. Worse still, it now seems like you need about half a dozen boxes of technology hanging off your television just to watch the football. Not a pretty sight, even when we're winning. Here's a project that uses some eyecatching fretwork to hide any eyesore electronics you have in your home.

1 Decide on the dimensions of your cabinet and the shelf heights, then cut out a shelf, the top and bottom panels, two side panels and one half-height back panel from MDF. Our cabinet was 1.2m (4ft) high, 90cm (3ft) wide and 60cm (2ft) deep, with a shelf halfway up, but you need to take into account the size of your television before you decide on the final dimensions for your project. *Glue/Screw* the outer carcass together and make sure it's all lying straight while it dries.

MATERIALS & EQUIPMENT

Tape measure
Pencil
2cm (¾in) MDF or ply (about two 2.4x1.2m (8x4ft) sheets)
Jigsaw with timber-cutting blade
Drill with 10mm wood bit for jigsaw pilot hole
Wood glue
3mm wood drill bit for pilot holes
4cm (1½in) size 8 wood screws
Screwdriver or screwdriver bit for drill
Spirit level with timber straight edge
2 hardboard fretwork panels (big enough for
   each door)
1.25cm (½in) panel pins
Hammer
4 concealed adjustable hinges
About 1.2m (4ft) of 5x2.5cm (2x1in) timber
   (for shelf battens)

Once you've made cupboards on this scale, you can let your ambitions grow. A little bigger and you have a decent crockery cupboard. Bigger still and you have a wardrobe. Bigger again and you have a very unusual garage...

2 Meanwhile, measure the width and height of the front of your cabinet and cut more MDF to create the two front doors. Mark a line about 7.5cm (3in) in from the sides and 10cm (4in) in from the top and bottom of the doors. (These measurements are just a guide as it really does depend on the size of your door as to what will look right.) Cut out the marked areas with a jigsaw, as this is where the fretwork will appear.

3 Measure and cut your fretwork panels 1.25cm (½in) larger than these openings in the doors, then attach the fretwork from the back with panel pins.

4 Glue/Screw the half-height panel on to the back of the cabinet to firm up the carcass. It's best to leave the bottom of the cabinet without a back so that you can get to all those wires when the video breaks down.

5 Use the concealed hinges, usually found on kitchen units, to attach the two doors. Screw two hinges on to each door about 20cm (8in) from the top and bottom. Once screwed into place, these hinges are adjustable to allow you to line up the doors so that they're exactly straight and level.

6 Finally, cut out three timber battens and *Glue/Screw* them to the inside of your cabinet, halfway up the side panels and to the back panel. These are to rest your shelf on. Glue and then pin the shelf in place. Ideally, this shelf should be no lower than the bottom of your half-height back panel so that you have three sides to support it. Still, it's your TV that's going to be resting on it...

scrap timber coffee table

If you have nowhere to put your scrap timber and nowhere to put your coffee, this could well be the ideal project for you. I think it looks great made out of rough-finished planks, but you could always make the table out of proper planed timber if you prefer. Feel free to alter the length of the legs of this project to produce a finished table that is perfectly suited to the level of seating which surrounds it.

1 Decide on the dimensions of your finished table and cut enough planks of 15x5cm (6x2in) timber to create the top. Glue the planks side by side. Secure this arrangement with a couple of timber battens 60cm (2ft) long screwed in from underneath, about 10cm (4in) from each end.

The simple construction techniques of this idea give you a straightforward way of making a very strong table. A project like this can easily be expanded to create either a low play table for the kids, or even a grown-up dining table for the adults. You can even allow two of the legs to come up through the surface to create the basis of chairs to match. Go wild...

BRIGHT IDEAS

If you've made this table out of scrap timber, the good news is that it's supposed to look rough and unfinished. If you've made it out of good stuff, I'm afraid you'll have to at least rub in some Danish Oil to protect the surface.

2 Measure and cut 2 pieces of 15x2.5cm (6x1in) timber the same length as your table-top and another 2 pieces 5cm (2in) wider than the width. Use 3 or 4 screws on each side to *Glue/Screw* these into place around the edge of your table-top to form a surround.

MATERIALS & EQUIPMENT

Tape measure
Pencil
15x5cm (6x2in) scrap timber
   (to create a table-top about
   120x60cm (4x2ft)
Handsaw or jigsaw with timber-
   cutting blade
Wood glue
About 1.2m (4ft) of 5x2.5cm
   (2x1in) timber batten
Bradawl or drill with 3mm wood
   bit for pilot holes
4.5cm (1¾in) size 8 wood screws
Screwdriver or screwdriver bit for
   drill
15x2.5cm (6x1in) timber (for
   table surround)
7.5x7.5cm (3x3in) timber
   (enough to make four 45cm
   (18in) legs)

3 Cut 4 table legs 45cm (18in) high from 7.5x7.5cm (3x3in) timber. This is the height you want your finished table, minus the thickness of the top, 5cm (2in). Most importantly, each leg should be exactly the same length! *Glue/Screw* the legs on to the inside of the surround at each corner, using 4 screws in each leg for strength. Turn it over and you're done. Two sugars in mine please.

room divider screen

You don't have to start building internal walls just to break a large room up into more habitable spaces. A simple room divider has many advantages. It's quick to knock up, even quicker to knock down and you can move it around whenever you're bored with the effect. Better still, it provides two more willing surfaces on which to demonstrate your masterful decorating skills.

MATERIALS & EQUIPMENT

Tape measure
Pencil
2cm (¾in) MDF or ply (about two 2.4x1.2m
  (8x4ft) sheets)
Compass (optional) made from a 60cm (2ft)
  piece of scrap timber batten and a nail at
  least 4cm (1½in) long, or string and a pencil
Hammer
Jigsaw with timber-cutting blade
6 flush hinges or piano hinges and screws
Bradawl
Screwdriver

1 Decide on the height and width of your screen then measure and cut three identical panels from the MDF or ply. If you want a semi-circular shape at the top of each panel, the quickest way to mark out your cutting line is to use a bit of old timber or some string as a compass. To do this, find the centre of the panel across its width and either nail in one end of the timber batten or anchor a piece of string with a nail. Using a pencil held at the free end of the timber or string, draw a semi-circle at the top of a panel.

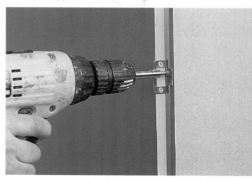

2 Screw three hinges to the edges of two panels to be joined, one in the middle and the other two 30cm (12in) from the top and bottom. Remember to fit the hinges so that the panels fold in alternate directions, like a zigzag snake. If you don't, your room divider will quickly become a very large box – not ideal.

Room dividers are dead trendy at the moment, so feel free to decorate them as you see fit. Paint them, paper them, cover them in fabric, whatever takes your fancy. And don't worry if you haven't actually got a room that needs dividing: just stick the divider in a corner with a lamp on the floor behind it and you'll have a magical drop of light in any room.

HANDY ANDY'S HOT TIPS
The semi-circular cut I created for the top of this screen is quick and easy to achieve, but if you want to spend slightly longer on the design to produce something rather more elaborate, you can always draw up an intricate paper template and use that to trace off a cut line on to the top of each panel.

all-purpose storage boxes

Most people assume that 'storage' means 'hiding'. That doesn't always need to be the case. This project will not only give you plenty of space to dump toys, magazines, videos, CDs and the like, but provide you with somewhere nice to sit or put your feet up into the bargain.

In the TV series, we used these storage boxes in a reception room, but I'll tell you where else they'd be very well received – the children's bedrooms. Paint them to look like castles and dolls' houses, or make a set of three to resemble the little pigs' houses, then cover them with something wild and wacky, such as fur fabric or astroturf. If your kids don't love them, you can always pop them inside.

HANDY ANDY'S HOT TIPS

The construction technique for this project produces a pretty strong box that can easily be scaled up to twice the size if you need the additional space. If your storage requirements are a bit more fluid, why not think about making a set of these boxes where each one is slightly smaller than the last? When you don't need the storage capacity any more, they will stack away inside each other just like a set of Russian dolls.

1 Decide on the dimensions of your finished box and cut all four sides, plus the top and bottom, from MDF or ply. Our box was 46cm (18in) wide, 41cm (16in) high and 36cm (14in) deep. The top needs to be the same size as the outer dimensions of the box, while the bottom should be 2cm (¾in) smaller all round. *Glue/Screw* timber battens to the inside corners, but make sure these stop well before what will be the bottom of the box. The distance you need to leave at the bottom will depend on the combined height of your castors and base panel. The battens should be placed so that the base panel rests against them with its castors sticking out about 5mm (¼in) underneath.

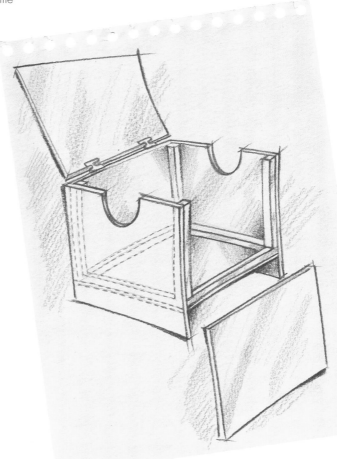

MATERIALS & EQUIPMENT

Tape measure
Pencil
2cm (¾in) MDF or ply (about one 1.2x1.2m (4x4ft) sheet per box)
Handsaw or jigsaw with timber-cutting blade
Wood glue
About 1.8m (6ft) of 2.5x2.5cm (1x1in) timber batten per box
Drill with 3mm wood bit for pilot holes
Screwdriver or screwdriver bit for drill
4 castors and screws per box
2 flush hinges and screws per box

3 Insert the base panel so that it rests against the horizontal battens you've just fixed. *Glue/Screw* it into position.

2 *Glue/Screw* the four sides together by screwing through the timber battens into the MDF side panels. Cut four more horizontal battens to fit between the vertical battens: these will support the base panel. *Glue/Screw* these to the sides of the box.

HANDY ANDY'S HOT TIPS

If you want to upholster the lid as the *Changing Rooms* designer Laurence Llewelyn-Bowen did in the series, you can cover some foam with fabric and just glue it into place.

4 Screw four castors on to the underside of the base panel in each corner, about 2.5cm (1in) away from the sides. If you measured everything correctly, the castors will protrude about 5mm (¼in) underneath. If you didn't, they won't.

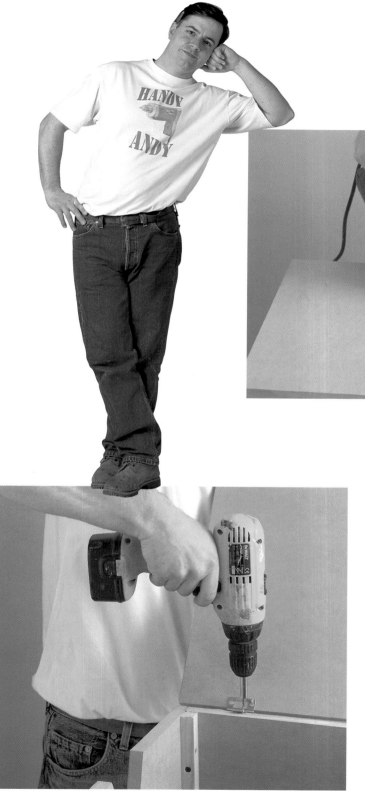

5 Mark hand-holes on the sides of the box, then cut them out. Mine were V-shaped, but you can make them any shape you like, just so long as you can eventually get your fingers in to open the lid.

6 Screw two flush hinges to the top back of the box and the lid, and you're done. Don't, however, assume that this is the easy bit. Make sure everything is lined up correctly before you mark and screw in any hinges and then check again.

scrap timber seat

This is more like it – some real carpentry to get your teeth into and a fabulous-looking piece of furniture when you've finished, but don't be tempted by the safe option on this one, the more adventurous you are with your design, the more delighted you'll be when it's finished. Always remember, however this project turns out, you can be assured of one thing – no one else is going to have a bench quite like yours.

1 Measure and mark out four legs of different heights on your 7.5x7.5cm (3x3in) timber: they should range from 90cm (3ft) to 150cm (5ft) high. Draw an ornate shape at the top of each leg, then cut round it with a jigsaw and drill a hole through it using a drill and 10mm wood bit. Decide on the depth of your finished bench and cut two cross-pieces of 5x5cm (2x2in) timber so that they are 10cm (4in) shorter than this dimension. Mark the height you want your seat to be off the ground, then use a tenon saw and chisel to cut 2.5cm (1in) slots into the legs. These slots should be high enough and wide enough to take the ends of the cross-pieces. Use glue and screws to secure the cross-pieces in place and so join the legs in pairs.

MATERIALS & EQUIPMENT

Tape measure
Pencil
About 6m (20ft) of 7.5x7.5cm (3x3in)
    scrap timber for the seat legs
Jigsaw with conventional timber blade and
    scroll-cutting blade
Drill with 10mm wood bit for decorative holes
About 3m (10ft) of 5x5cm (2x2in) scrap timber
    for the cross-pieces
Tenon saw
2.5cm (1in) bevel-edged chisel
Wood glue
3mm wood bit for pilot holes
7.5cm (3in) size 8 wood screws
Screwdriver or screwdriver bit for drill
About 9m (30ft) of 10x2.5cm (4x1in) timber
    for the arms, back and seat
2.5cm (1in) spade bit for mortise holes
Sandpaper
4cm (1½in) lost head nails
Hammer
Nail punch

The construction principles of this project are sound at any scale. Whether you're after an ornate armchair or a three-seater sofa, this idea will kit you out with all the skills you need. The only thing to watch is the thickness of your cross-pieces: the longer the sofa, the thicker these will need to be.

2 Decide on the width of your finished bench and cut two more cross-pieces that are 10cm (4in) shorter than this dimension. Cut four more 2.5cm (1in) slots in the legs the same size and height as before and use more glue and screws to insert the third and fourth cross-piece, thus joining all the legs firmly together.

3 The arms can be cut from any scrap timber about 10x2.5cm (4x1in). They should be about 2.5cm (1in) longer than the gap between the inside edges of the front and back legs on each side. Work out the most comfortable height for each arm, then use the 2.5cm (1in) spade bit followed by the chisel to drill and smooth out 1cm (½in) deep slots in the centre of each leg. These slots should be 10x2.5cm (4x1in) so that the ends of the arms will *Glue/Screw* snugly into place. The back cross-piece can be cut and secured in a similar way, but it's probably best to fix it a few inches higher than the arms.

4 For the seat itself, cut planks to match the length of your bench and saw out the corners where the front and back planks meet the legs. *Glue/Screw* these planks on to the cross-pieces – they don't really need to be secured to each other. Make sure you sand them down well because splinters here would be a real pain in the… seat. Using the same size of timber, cut a length for the back cross-piece. This should be about 2.5cm (1in) longer than the gap between the back two legs. Mark its position about 50cm (20in) above the seat, then cut slots for it in each back leg: these should be 1cm (½in) deep with a 10x2.5cm (4x1in) opening. *Glue/Screw* the back cross-piece into place.

BRIGHT IDEAS

For an even more decorative appearance to your bench, you can use the drill or jigsaw to create more designs in the side and rear cross-pieces.

5 Mark out fancy shapes on your timber for the uprights at the back of the bench, then cut them out with a jigsaw. They should fit exactly between the seat and the underside of the back cross-piece. The design of these uprights can be as wild as you like. The beauty of this bench is that it's actually meant to look a bit rough around the edges. Magic!

6 Stick the uprights in place using plenty of wood glue, then hammer in panel pins at an angle to hold everything securely while the glue dries. Make sure the uprights are evenly spaced across the back of the bench.

star cupboard doors

Give the star treatment to a forgotten alcove. This quick and clever idea for a cupboard can be adapted to any size of opening, and the motif you choose for decoration can be as simple or elaborate as you wish. If you want, you can always add some shelves or a curtain rail behind the doors to accommodate all your stuff.

MATERIALS & EQUIPMENT

Tape measure
Pencil
5x2.5cm (2x1in) timber batten (enough to go all round the alcove)
Jigsaw with timber-cutting blade
Drill with 6mm masonry bit
Bradawl
6mm wall plugs (solid or cavity)
3mm wood drill bit for pilot holes
4.5cm (1¾in) size 8 wood screws (for battens)
Screwdriver or screwdriver drill bit
2cm (¾in) MDF or ply (about two 2.4x1.2m (8x4ft) sheets)
Paper for template
10mm wood drill bit for jigsaw pilot holes
4 concealed adjustable hinges
5cm (2in) size 8 wood screws (for handles)
Wood glue

1 Measure the height of your alcove, then cut corresponding lengths of timber battens. Secure the battens down the sides and along the top and bottom of the alcove. (Those at top and bottom should act as backstops for the doors when they are closed.) *Plug/Screw* the battens to the walls and ceiling, but simply screw into the floor if it's wood.

If you really want to be flash with this project, think about securing some little fretwork or punched metal panels behind the openings in each door. Then, if you've got a handy plug socket, fix a light in the cupboard so that it shines out through the holes in the doors. Finally, wait until nightfall, then sit back and contemplate how brilliant you are at DIY.

HANDY ANDY'S HOT TIPS

You don't have to use stars as the motif on your cupboard. If you want to be more adventurous, you could use moons, comets, or even space rockets. In fact, if you have a motif in your room featured in the fabric, the wallpaper or even the carpet around you (a flower or *fleur de lys* for example) then why not take that as your inspiration and make a paper template to copy it onto the cupboard doors.

2 Measure the height and width of your alcove then cut 2 doors from MDF or ply to fit. Make a paper template of a star shape, then trace round it in the same position on each door. Make a hole in the stars using a 10mm drill bit, then insert your jigsaw blade and carefully cut out the shapes.

3 Hang the doors, using two concealed adjustable hinges on each door. They should be positioned about 50cm (20in) from the top and bottom. Adjust the hinges to make sure the doors hang straight and level.

4 Use your paper template again to mark out two more star shapes on some spare bits of timber.

5 These are going to form the handles for the doors. Place a little square of timber behind the stars to hold your handles away from the doors. *Glue/Screw* everything in place, but make sure you do this fixing from the back so that no screw heads are left on show.

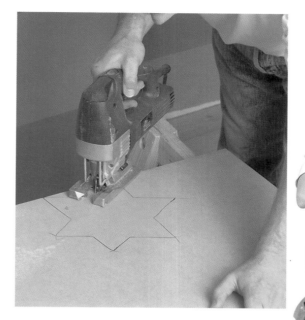

BRIGHT IDEAS

If you are particularly careful when you drill and cut the cupboard doors to remove the star shapes from their openings, you might well find that you can use these self-same cut-outs as the handles. If you're short on timber, every little helps...

KITCHENS &
BATHROOMS

Not so long ago the kitchen was simply a part of the house where you prepared your meals, and the bathroom was a part of the house where you 'powdered your nose'. Thankfully our attitude towards these rooms has changed in recent years. Nowadays the kitchen and bathrooms are as much the focus of elaborate design and decoration as receptions rooms have always been. Indeed, estate agents will tell you that it's kitchens and bathrooms that now sell the properties, so get your teeth stuck into these exciting homebuilt projects…

lino-tiled floor

I can still remember the days when lino was what you put on the floor when you couldn't afford anything better. How things have changed! You can now get amazing designs in this rugged and practical material, and, best of all, the only tools you need to lay it are a hammer, a pencil and a sharp knife. *Changing Rooms* designer Laurence Llewelyn-Bowen chose elegant white lino tiles for this project, but you can pick any colour you like.

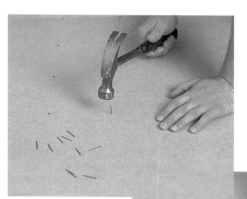

HANDY ANDY'S HOT TIPS

The temptation when you're laying tiles is just to start from one long wall and work outwards. Unfortunately, even modern houses have rooms that can stray a long way from perfect 90° corners, and if you simply lay tiles from one side to another, your precious new floor can look like it's been laid by someone with very wonky eyesight. Sadly, you won't even realize the full extent of the mistake until you've completely finished and everything's stuck down... Far better to start your pattern right in the middle of the floor and cope with the slants at each wall when you come to them.

1 Preparation is everything in this project. Clear the room and measure the floor area. Check the floorboards and hammer down any large nail heads or staples. Also make sure any loose or rotten boards are secured or replaced. Now cut and lay pieces of hardboard or thin ply across the whole floor area and secure in place with panel pins. The ply needs to be secured at least every 15cm (6in) – tedious but necessary, I'm afraid, to ensure evenness.

2 Find the middle of all four walls, stretch a length of string between opposite points and draw a line across, following the string. You should end up with a big cross right in the centre of the floor. Start laying your tiles at this central point and work out towards the edges of the room.

MATERIALS & EQUIPMENT

Tape measure
Pencil
Hammer
Nail punch
Hardboard or thin ply (enough to cover the floor area)
Handsaw or jigsaw with timber-cutting blade
1cm (⅓in) panel pins
String (long enough to reach across the room)
Self-adhesive lino tiles (enough to cover the floor area)
Paper for template
Craft knife

Remember, tiles are not just for flat floors. If you like the effect they produce in your room, you can continue your design up the front of steps, up the sides of a bath or even over a cupboard door.

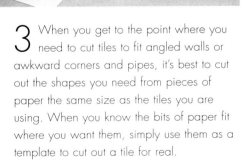

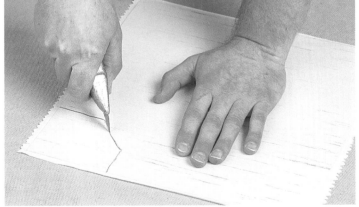

3 When you get to the point where you need to cut tiles to fit angled walls or awkward corners and pipes, it's best to cut out the shapes you need from pieces of paper the same size as the tiles you are using. When you know the bits of paper fit where you want them, simply use them as a template to cut out a tile for real.

4 Always use a very sharp knife to cut through the tiles. It's blunt knives that cause all the accidents, as you repeatedly scrape away trying to get a clean cut all the way through.

fake flagstone floor

Now some things in this book are pretty clever, but some things are just brilliant. Here's one of them. Real stone flooring can break the bank in more ways than one. Unless you happen to have a quarry behind your house, it can all get far too expensive, and if you don't have some fairly substantial joints underneath, it can all get far too heavy! This project uses something called self-levelling floor compound to give you a quick and cheap alternative to genuine stone flooring.

1 Clear the room and sweep the floor clean of all dust and debris. The floor should be absolutely solid, so if it's not made of concrete, you'll have to measure it up, then lay down hardboard sheets and secure them every 15cm (6in) with panel pins – boring, but well worth it in the end. Now mix up a batch of self-levelling compound according to the manufacturer's instructions and pour it over the floor. (One batch should make about 4 square yards of floor.) Always work from the far end of the room towards the door, unless you're planning to sleep in there overnight…

MATERIALS & EQUIPMENT

Tape measure
Pencil
Hardboard or thin ply (enough to cover the floor area)
Handsaw or jigsaw with timber-cutting blade
1cm (½in) panel pins
Hammer
Self-levelling floor compound (no more than 4mm (¼in) deep all over)
Plasterer's trowel

If your floor is going to take a lot of traffic, it's probably a good idea to protect it. We painted ours with emulsion to make it a more interesting colour, then applied a few coats of acrylic varnish. This not only increases the life of the self-levelling compound, it also makes the floor much easier to clean when you spill something on it.

2 Once you've started, you'll need to complete the whole room in one go so that you don't get any odd lines running through the surface of the compound. However, don't be tempted to smooth out the surface too evenly – it does a lot of levelling on its own. (There's a clue in the name.) Use a plasterer's trowel to spread the compound and don't be afraid to leave the odd mark in it: it's supposed to look like real stone, after all.

3 After 1–2 hours, depending on the air temperature, use a stick or the edge of the trowel to lightly score the lines of imaginary flagstones. Our flagstones were about 30x38cm (12x15in) in size. Re-score the lines when the compound is firm enough to walk on but not completely set. Always remember that old designer cop-out: 'It's meant to look a bit rough; that's just how I wanted it.'

punched-metal doors

These cupboard doors look tremendous when they're finished, but be warned – this is not a quick project. If you don't want to be punching holes all night, limit your designs to a fairly simple pattern that you plan out in advance. However, that aspect aside, if you're looking to revamp some tired old cupboard doors you'd be hard pressed to find a more effective and exciting technique than this.

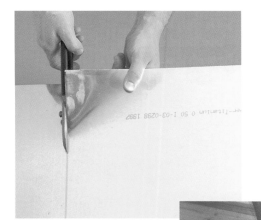

1 Take off your old cupboard doors and lay them on a flat surface. Measure the front of them and cut matching zinc panels 2.5cm (1in) smaller all round. Use proper tin snips to cut the zinc and watch your fingers on the sharp edges.

2 Now measure and cut 5cm (2in) strips of 0.5cm (¼in) MDF to fit all around the outer edges of the zinc panels. You can mitre or flat join these strips (see page 30), depending on how much time you have. Turn over all the MDF strips, remembering what fits where, then use a ruler and pencil to mark out a rebate 2.5cm (1in) wide on what will become the inside edge of the rear face. Use a plane to slice out a rebate just deep enough to accommodate the zinc panel.

MATERIALS & EQUIPMENT

Screwdriver or drill with screw
   driver bit
Tape measure
Pencil
Zinc sheeting (enough to cover
   your doors)
Tin snips
0.5cm (¼in) MDF or ply
   (enough to create 5cm (2in)
   strips all around your doors)
Handsaw or jigsaw with timber-
   cutting blade
Mitre block (optional)
Electric or hand plane
Paper for template
Non-fast felt pen
Hammer
Large nail (for punching holes)
Wood glue
3mm wood bit for pilot holes
1.5cm (½in) size 8 wood screws

The sunshine pattern chosen for these doors was designed to fit in with a Mexican kitchen, but you can use whatever motif you like. Browse through books or magazines for inspiration, and if you're worried about your artistic ability, simply photocopy your chosen pictures, enlarging them to the size you want. Just tape down the photocopy and punch through the paper.

3 Make a paper template of your design, then use a washable felt pen to mark it on to the zinc panels. Use a nail and hammer to punch it out. Remember, however detailed your first panel is, all the others will have to match. Start on something wildly ornate and your children will probably inherit the project.

4 Place your new panels in the centre of the old doors and secure them in place by *Glue/Screwing* the strips of MDF to the old doors so that the zinc sits neatly in the rebates you planed out. Re-fit the doors and get medical attention for the thumb you hit about 500 times while punching the metal.

tongue-and-groove-effect doors

Tired of looking at the same old cupboard doors? Here's a make-over project that will transform them into something that looks as though it's lovingly crafted from expensive tongue-and-groove timber planks instead of knocked up out of cheap and cheerful MDF.

1 Remove the existing cupboard doors, place them on the sheet of MDF and mark out panels to cover them exactly.

MATERIALS & EQUIPMENT

Screwdriver or drill with screwdriver bit
1.25cm (½in) MDF or ply (enough to cover your doors)
Pencil
Handsaw or jigsaw with timber-cutting blade
Tape measure
Timber straight edge
Router with V-profile bit
2 clamps (to hold straight edge in place for router)
Wood glue
2.5cm (1in) size 8 wood screws
3mm wood bit for pilot holes

2 Cut out the MDF panels, then measure and mark evenly spaced vertical lines down the front about 10cm (4in) apart using a timber straight edge. Clamp the straight edge in place next to the first line, then use a router with a V-shaped bit to cut a light groove from the top to the bottom of the panel. Repeat this process with all the lines on each panel.

I love the look of tongue-and-groove timber. Once you've got the knack of this quick trick to simulate the real thing, you'll find you can use them in many different situations: on the floor, for a trendy nautical feel; on the walls, for some Shaker-style chic; even on the ceiling, for a swish Nordic bathroom. Rubbed down or painted up, a few coats of varnish will make the surface suitable for use in any room you like.

3 Glue the finished MDF panels into place on the old doors and secure with screws put in from behind. Finally, re-fit the doors and finish them off with some nice new handles.

BRIGHT IDEAS

If you don't want the additional weight and thickness this project adds to your existing cupboard units, you could always use the MDF as a complete replacement for the old doors. Simply make sure your MDF is the same thickness as the old doors it's replacing, cut out and router in the normal way, then transfer all the hinge mechanisms to re-hang the doors in their original position.

chalet shutters

Tired of curtains? Weary of blinds? Fed up with the neighbours peering in all day long? Learn a lesson from Switzerland without even leaving the house. These chalet-style shutters are all the rage in countries where the snow piles up against the house, but there's no reason why you can't have them over here as well.

The project uses a fair amount of timber, but the end result is stunning and well worth the expense. It is also a particularly attractive and effective way of reducing the noise from a busy road at night.

MATERIALS & EQUIPMENT

Tape measure
Pencil
10cm (4in) tongue-and-groove planks (enough to cover your window with a maximum of four shutters)
Handsaw or jigsaw with timber-cutting blade
Wood glue
7.5x2.5cm (3 x1in) planed timber (3.5 times as wide as your window)
Sliding bevel
Bradawl or drill with 3mm wood bit for pilot holes
4cm (1½in) size 8 wood screws
Screwdriver or screwdriver bit for drill
2.5x2.5cm (1x1in) timber batten (twice the height of your window)
Spirit level with timber straight edge
6mm masonry bit
6mm wall plugs (solid or cavity)
5cm (2in) size 10 wood screws
4x23cm (9in) 'T'-shaped hinges
1cm (½in) size 8 wood screws
2.5cm (1in) size 8 wood screws
Sash clamps (optional)

1 Measure the height and width of your window, then calculate the dimensions of 2 equal-sized doors to fit the space. (They should be no wider than about 80cm (2ft 8in) each, so if your window is more than about 160cm (5ft) across, you'll have to span the gap with 4 doors instead of 3. See Handy Andy's Hot Tips for further information.) Cut 10cm (4in) tongue-and-groove planks to create the doors, then fit each of them together with glue down every groove. Leave to dry for a couple of hours while you get on with step 2.

These shutters can transform the most boring window into quite a feature, especially if you add a dramatic splash of colour with some bold paint. Furthermore, you can enlarge the whole project to provide full-length shutters for patio doors – the construction method remains exactly the same.

2 On what will be the inside of each door, create a bracing Z-shape from 7.5x2.5cm (3 x1in) planed timber to add strength and rigidity to the doors. The two horizontal braces should be about 15cm (6in) from the top and bottom of the shutter. *Glue/Screw* into position with 4cm (1½in) size 8 screws.

3 Measure and mitre your diagonal battens so that they fit snugly against the horizontal battens. *Glue/Screw* into position using more 4cm (1½in) size 8 screws. This is the side of the shutter that you'll have to look at when it's closed, so make a nice job of it.

BRIGHT IDEAS

For that ultimate chalet chic you could cut some decorative little shapes out of the shutters before you put them up. Diamond cut-outs always look neat, but you could attempt *fleur de lys* if you have the patience to cut a more complicated shape. Use a size 10 drill bit to make a starter hole for the jigsaw blade, but make sure you drill into an area of the wood that you'll be cutting out! Cut the shapes so that they are about eye level when the shutters are in place and you'll find they make perfect little peepholes when the neighbours are on form.

4 Measure and cut 2 vertical battens from 2.5x2.5cm (1x1in) timber for the wall on each side of the window. They should be exactly the same length as the shutters, i.e. the height of the window. *Plug/Screw* them into position with 5cm (2in) size 10 wood screws. Make sure these battens are very strong as all the weight of the finished shutters will be hanging from them 24 hours a day. They will be under particular strain near the top, so make sure you secure them every 15cm (6in). If in doubt about their strength, upgrade your wall battens to 5x2.5cm (2x1in) timber and put in some more screws for good measure.

HANDY ANDY'S HOT TIPS

You can cover fairly wide windows by making your shutters in a set of four rather than two. Just use four more 23cm (9in) 'T' hinges to attach the third and fourth doors, placing the hinges on the braced side this time so that the doors will fold in on themselves when open. If you are making a wider construction like this, take even more care when attaching your vertical battens to the wall: they need to be held firmly in place, and don't try to cover windows any wider than about 3m (10 feet). As a final touch you could add some decorative bolts or latches to the shutters to hold them tightly closed.

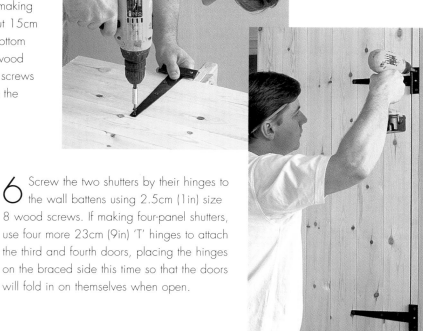

5 Screw a couple of 23cm (9in) 'T' hinges to the unbraced side of the shutters (the first two shutters only, if making four). Position them about 15cm (6in) from the top and bottom using 1cm (½in) size 8 wood screws. Make sure your screws don't go right through to the other side.

6 Screw the two shutters by their hinges to the wall battens using 2.5cm (1in) size 8 wood screws. If making four-panel shutters, use four more 23cm (9in) 'T' hinges to attach the third and fourth doors, placing the hinges on the braced side this time so that the doors will fold in on themselves when open.

ornate chair backs

Now, everybody knows that you can revamp old floors, old walls and even old cupboards, but what about your furniture? Here's a project that will turn a sad old seat into a trendy new designer dining chair. And if you've ever been keen to try out a bit of jigsawing, this will provide all the oppurtunity you could ever hope for.

MATERIALS & EQUIPMENT

Handsaw
Tape measure
Pencil
Paper for template
2.5cm (1in) MDF or ply (about 60x90cm (2x3ft) per chair)
Jigsaw with scroll-cutting blade

Wood glue
Drill with 3mm wood bit for pilot holes
4cm (1½in) size 8 wood screws
Screwdriver or screwdriver bit for drill
Sandpaper

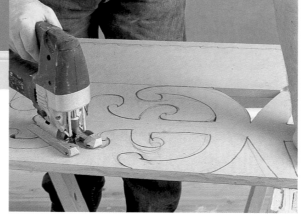

1 Find an old wooden chair with a boring design that you're tired of looking at. Use a handsaw or jigsaw to cut out the seat back, leaving the uprights intact.

2 Measure the gap you have left and decide how high you want the new back to be. Using a paper template, mark out a design on 2.5cm (1in) MDF to fit this gap and cut it out with a jigsaw. Make sure your design allows for the MDF to be attached to the uprights in at least two places on each side.

While you might be tempted to design your new chair back as a scale replica of the Eiffel Tower, just bear in mind who's going to be cutting it out. If it's you, play it simple and keep it easy to get round all the corners. If someone else is doing the work, I think the Eiffel Tower would look great…

3 *Glue/Screw* the new back to the existing uprights where the two touch. Drill pilot holes for the screws and ensure the screw heads lie flush with the surface. Sand down any rough edges before painting it.

HANDY ANDY'S HOT TIPS

As long as you have at least two points of contact on each side, you can make your new backs much higher than the old ones — right up to head height in fact. This is a clever way of turning boring old kitchen chairs into dramatic new dining room thrones. A fine coat of gold or silver paint, and you really will have something fit for a king.

tiled splashback

Now this is all a bit grown-up – real tiling, real splashback, real kitchen. Only problem is, it's your kitchen, so concentrate... This project is nowhere near as hard as you might imagine. Make sure you prepare for the job properly, make sure you've got the right tools and materials, and make sure you follow what I say. If you can manage that, then I guarantee you'll end up with a very impressive and very professional-looking splashback that will change the whole character of your existing kitchen.

1 Clean and smooth the surface of the wall to be tiled and loose-lay your tiles along the work surface at the bottom of it. This will help you to plan where to start and how you want the tiles to look. Don't forget to check with a spirit level that you're working along a straight edge.

MATERIALS & EQUIPMENT

Tiles (enough to cover area required)
Spirit level with timber straight edge
Ready-mixed or powdered tile adhesive
Adhesive spreader
Tile spacers (allow 2 per tile)
Tape measure

Pencil
Tile scribe or tile-cutting tool
Ready-mixed or powdered waterproof
  grout
Damp cloth
Masking tape
Silicone sealant and cartridge gun

Now that you have mastered the art of tiling, there's a world of walls out there just craving your attention. Even with large areas, such as bathrooms, the principles involved are just the same.

2 Spread on your adhesive a little bit at a time using a proper adhesive trowel. Work section by section (six tiles at a time) and don't move on until everything's perfect. Press your tiles into place and as you stick each one down, place a tile spacer at each corner so that every tile is evenly spaced from the surrounding tiles.

3 When you come to a point where a tile must be cut to fit, measure and mark very carefully before cutting. Always use a proper cutting tool to score and snap the tile (see page 84). If you're tiling a corner, use the piece you have just broken off to continue on to the next wall.

4 Once all the tiles are in place, cover the whole area with waterproof grout, making sure it fills the gaps between the tiles. Quickly wipe off any surplus grout with a damp cloth.

5 Put masking tape along the bottom of the tiled area where your tiling meets the work surface, then spread out a bead of silicone sealant to make this gap watertight.

6 Once the sealant's dry (after about 2 hours, but check manufacturer's instructions), peel off the masking tape. It's a good idea to run a sharp knife along the top edge of the sealant first to make sure there's no tearing when the tape is pulled away.

BRIGHT IDEAS

This project doesn't have to stop where the wall meets the worksurface. If your existing kitchen units are a little on the tired side, why not tile down the wall and right over your worktops as well? If the existing worksurface is a shiny plastic or formica finish, you should sand it down a bit to give the tile adhesive something to bond to.

scrap timber worksurface

Most modern kitchens come with fairly cheap and uninspiring worksurfaces. This project shows you how to change them into something far more attractive. The added bonus (if you're tall) is that it will also slightly raise the level of the worksurface, which will make it a lot more comfortable to work at. Always remember to give the wood a coat of acrylic varnish or Danish Oil before the fat really starts flying.

1 Measure your existing work-surface and cut tongue-and-groove flooring of either size listed to create a new worktop which is about 2.5cm (1in) bigger than the original all round. Glue the planks together and hold in place with sash clamps (see page 14) until everything is completely dry.

2 Use a handsaw to cut your new worksurface down to the exact size of the old one, losing any tongue edges or uneven ends to the planks in the process.

MATERIALS & EQUIPMENT

Tape measure
Pencil
10cm (4in) or 15cm (6in) tongue-and-groove floor planks (enough to create a worktop slightly larger than your existing one)
Handsaw or jigsaw with timber-cutting blade
Wood glue
Sash clamps
Drill with 3mm wood bit for pilot holes
4.5cm (1½in) size 8 wood screws
Screwdriver or screwdriver bit for drill
5x2.5cm (2x1in) timber batten (enough to go all along the front edge of the worktop)
4cm (1½in) panel pins
Hammer

If you like this project so much that you want to extend it right around the kitchen, go ahead. You can always cut holes in the new surface to accommodate the sink and cooker hob.

3 Glue the new worksurface to the old one and secure with screws from inside the cupboards. The screws shouldn't be so long that they pop up through the top.

4 Use lengths of 5x2.5cm (2x1in) timber batten to cover the new front edge of the worksurface and glue and panel pin them into position. If you like the effect, you can add more battens at the back, where the worksurface meets the wall.

fake wall panelling

This must qualify for the easiest cheat in the whole book. Proper panelled rooms look very flash indeed, but to make them for real takes forever. The stick-on beading strips we use here will turn a flat wall into a fake hall faster than you can say 'self-adhesive'. The product is known as 'Fake Victorian Door Panel Kit' and is available from most of the larger DIY stores as an easy way to make plain doors look older.

HANDY ANDY'S HOT TIPS

As these panel kits were originally designed for livening up plain doors, why not include the door of the room you're 'panelling' in your design? Even if you're not working on the walls, there's no quicker way to give your cupboard or wardrobe doors a lift than by a bit of instant panelling.

The way you space your panels will have a significant effect on the mood of your room. A lot of panels grouped tightly together will lend a busy and ornate feeling to the walls, while a looser arrangement with bigger gaps in between will create a much softer and understated impression.

1 Using a spirit level with a timber straight edge, carefully measure and mark up your walls to indicate where the fake panels are to go. These should be positioned evenly along the wall at regular intervals (see Handy Andy's Hot Tips). This is the hardest and the most important part. Bodge the measuring and everything will look a mess.

2 Now, simply peel off the backing paper and carefully stick your beading strips in place. That's it – they're done. You can paint over them as soon as you like.

MATERIALS & EQUIPMENT

Spirit level with timber straight
   edge
Tape measure
Pencil
Self-adhesive beading strips

BRIGHT IDEAS

Once in place these little panels are an invitation to add paint effects to the finished wall. Try painting the wall inside the beading a slightly different shade to the wall outside. A subtle difference in tone for cool and classy, a completely different colour for 'in your face' drama.

timber pot rack

It's amazing how much junk you need in the kitchen just to cook a simple meal. If your cupboards are spewing pots and pans every time you open a door, here's a practical and stylish solution to your over-crowding crisis. It also lets you hang your utensils near at hand rather than stuffed at the back of shelves and cupboards.

MATERIALS & EQUIPMENT

Tape measure
Pencil
7.5x2.5cm (3x1in) timber batten
   (about 3m (10ft) for a
   60x90cm (2x3ft) rack)
Handsaw or jigsaw with
   timber-cutting edge
Mitre block (optional)
Wood glue
4cm (1½in) panel pins or lost
   head nails
Hammer
Drill with 2.5cm (1in) spade bit
2.5cm (1in) wooden dowel or
   metal pipe (about 3.3m (11ft))
Screwdriver or screwdriver
   bit for drill
Bradawl
4 x 4cm (1½in) screw-in eyelets
Pliers
120cm (4ft) chain
3mm wood bit for pilot
   holes in ceiling
2 plasterboard fixing plugs
2 x 4cm (1½in) screw-in
   hooks

We left our pot rack in the natural timber with just a coat of varnish for protection, but if your kitchen cries out for a more high-tech or colourful finish then you can use either metallic spray paints or acrylic wood paints to transform your finished rack into something far more dynamic.

BRIGHT IDEAS

If you really want to impress the family, you could make your end battens curved rather than straight so that the finished rack appears to bow downwards (see Andy's sketch). These curved end battens would need to be jigsawed from a larger piece of wood and would benefit from a more elaborate mortise and tenon technique (see page 31) to secure them in place, but a butt joint would suffice. Apart from looking flash, the curve of the finished rack means you could hang objects of different sizes all at the same height.

1 Measure and cut lengths of 7.5x2.5cm (3x1in) timber batten to create an outer frame of the size you require. We cut two lengths 60cm (2ft) long and two lengths 90cm (3ft) long for our pot rack. Mitre the corners if you feel up to it; otherwise, use butt joints (see page 30) if you want to simplify the project. Glue and panel pin the corners together to secure the frame. Wait for the glue to dry completely before going on to the next step.

2 Drill three evenly spaced holes through each short side of the frame, using a spade bit. The size of the bit should correspond to the diameter of the dowelling poles.

HANDY ANDY'S HOT TIPS

This project is designed to hang from the ceiling, but you can use the same construction technique to produce something that will screw to the wall, or even slot into the top of an existing cupboard or open shelving unit. If you have lots of junk you need to hang up, just increase the frame size to fit in more poles to hang things from.

3 Cut three poles or pipes so that they're about 5cm (2in) longer than the length of the pot rack. Fit these poles into the frame with glue or screws so that they can't fall out. If using glue, leave it to dry for as long as specified on the tube, and keep the frame on a flat surface to ensure that it all stays straight. If using screws, drive them through the frame and into the poles from above.

4 Make pilot holes at each top corner of the frame and insert screw-in eyelets using pliers. Attach lengths of chain to the eyelets. Drill two holes in the ceiling, preferably into a joist, and insert the screw-in hooks. If you can't find a joist, insert plasterboard plugs for the hooks. Suspend the frame from the hooks and get hanging.

safe as houses

It is a well-known fact that the majority of accidents happen in the home. It is less well known that it is usually my home they happen in, but that still leaves some statistics left over for you if you're not careful. The first and most obvious piece of advice I can give you is always to read the manufacturer's notes on any of the tools or materials you are using. They don't supply all that information just to make the box or leaflet look busy – it's there for a reason, and the chances are that the reason is because someone has already made the mistake they are trying to warn you against.

Even when things don't come with specific safety instructions, it's in your own interest to use a large helping of common sense when you work. For instance, anything with a blade is designed to cut things and it won't be at all fussy about what that thing is. Knife blades and chisels like nothing better than a bit of finger when they get the chance, so always work them away from your body. If they slip, and one day they will, you want them to be slipping into fresh air, not fresh meat. Also, keep your knife blades and chisels sharp: that way they'll be far more tempted to cut what you're pointing them at rather than wandering off for something softer, such as your leg.

Working with power tools brings in a whole new raft of concerns, not least of which is electricity itself. It's always safest to use a circuit breaker plug between your power socket and your power tools. If anything goes wrong with the supply or with the wiring in your electric drill/saw/sander, the circuit breaker will know about it (and do something) long before you get the chance to find out the hard way. Always be aware of where the flex from your power tool is trailing: on the floor behind you is good, hidden under the wood you are cutting in front of you is bad. And when buying power equipment make sure that it displays the kitemark (the British Standards mark of safety). If, however, you can remember only one piece of advice at a time, make it this. Never switch anything on until you know how to switch it off.

When you are drilling holes into the walls of your house, remember that it's not all brick and plaster in there. Hidden all over the house are water pipes and electrical cables. For the most part, plumbing is usually under the floorboards or concentrated around your boiler and water tanks, but lighting and socket cables are much more widespread. Steer clear of drilling immediately around either light switches or wall sockets and you should be fine. If you are still in any doubt, you can buy little detector devices from most DIY stores, which warn you of pipes and cables just below the surface of your walls.

When using an electric drill or saw, always make sure you have fitted the correct drill bit or blade for the material you are working with and that it is not too old or damaged to work properly. If you need to force the tool into the material, there's something wrong, and more pushing is only going to make it worse.

It sounds obvious, but be careful not to remove the drill, saw or power sander from the material until it has stopped. Not only is it particularly dangerous to have a power tool waving around in the open while still going at full tilt, it is also the best way to ruin an otherwise perfect hole or saw cut. Always try to let the tools calm down completely before you pull them off the job in hand. Also, whenever we mess around with lighting or electrical equipment in the TV series, it is done by a qualified electrician. None of us can be geniuses at everything, so don't be too proud to consult an expert: always get an electrician to check any electrical equipment that has recently been installed.

Finally, all DIY projects create waste materials or fumes, and the worst way to dispose of them is by using your eyes, nose, mouth and skin to soak them up. If using power saws or power drills, it's always safest to wear protective goggles. Believe me, you look a lot more stupid with slivers of wood in your eyes than a pair of goggles over them. If using a power sander or cutting MDF, you should definitely wear a face mask to keep all the dust out of your nose and mouth. Also, it's always best to do your fabrication work in bright, well-ventilated conditions, such as your garden. There's more fresh air out there and less sweeping up to do afterwards.

suppliers of DIY materials and equipment

FOR LOCAL DIY STORES

B&Q plc
Portswood House
1 Hampshire Corporate
Park
Chandler's Ford
Hampshire
SO53 3YX
01703 256256

Do It All Helpline
West Street
Off Stafford Road
Wolverhampton
West Midlands
WV10 6HT
Freephone 0500 300321

Great Mills Retail Limited
RMC House
Paulton
Bristol
BS39 7SX
01761 416034

Homebase Limited
Beddington House
Railway Approach
Wallington
Surrey
SM6 0HB
0181 784 7200

Wickes Building Supplies
Limited
Station Road
Harrow
Middlesex
HA1 2QB
Freephone 0500 300328
Customer Enquiries 0870
6089001

FOR LOCAL HIRE SHOPS

HSS Hire Shops
1–3 Western House Road
Trafford Park
Manchester
M17 1PQ
0800 282 8282

POWER TOOL ENQUIRIES

Black and Decker
BMJ Power
Unit 15, Field Drive
West Cross Centre
Great West Road
Brentford
TW8 9EX
0345 230230

Bosch Limited
PO Box 98
Broadwater Park
Denham
Middlesex
UB9 5HJ
01895 838743

GENERAL TOOL ENQUIRIES

Buck and Ryan Limited
101 Tottenham Court
Road
London
W1P 0DY
0171 636 7475

Draper Tools
Hursley Road
Chandler's Ford
Eastleigh
Hants
SO53 1YF
01703 266355

Stanley Tools
Woodside
Sheffield
S3 9PD
0114 276 8888

WALL PLUGS AND TILE TOOLS

Plasplugs Limited
Wetmore Road
Burton-on-Trent
Staffordshire
DE14 1SD
01283 530303

Rawlplug Co Ltd
Glasgow
G46 8JR
0141 638 7961

FRETWORK SUPPLIERS

Jali Fretwork
Apsley House
Chartham
Canterbury
Kent
CT4 7HT
01227 831710

PLASTER CORBELS

Plasterworks
38 Cross Street
London
N1 2BG
0171 226 5355

ADHESIVE AND FILLER ENQUIRIES

Henkel Home
Improvement & Adhesive
Products
Winsford
Cheshire
CW7 3QY
01606 593933

PAINT ENQUIRIES

Crown Paints
PO Box 37
Crown House
Hollins Road
Darwen
Lancashire
BB3 0BG
01254 704951